Being Catholic

WHAT EVERY CATHOLIC SHOULD KNOW

Being Catholic

WHAT EVERY CATHOLIC SHOULD KNOW

Suzie Andres

IGNATIUS PRESS   AUGUSTINE INSTITUTE
San Francisco   Greenwood Village, CO

Cover Design: Davin Carlson

© 2020 Ignatius Press, San Francisco,
and the Augustine Institute, Greenwood Village, CO
All rights reserved
ISBN 978-1-7338598-9-9 (pbk)
ISBN 978-1-950939-16-9 (hbk)
ISBN 978-1-950939-40-4 (eBook)
Library of Congress Control Number 2020943394

Printed in Canada ∞

For Sanjay

O how glorious our Faith is!
Instead of restricting hearts, as the world fancies,
It uplifts them and enlarges their capacity to love.

— St. Thérèse of Lisieux

Contents

Introduction

On What You Will Find Herein

I have heard it said that G. K. Chesterton and Hilaire Belloc used to argue about whether it was better to be a convert, one who had chosen the Faith and could deeply appreciate it after years without the life-giving water and fullness of Truth, or to be a cradle Catholic who had the advantage of loving the Good, the True, and the Beautiful from infancy. Happily, many in our day have the blessing of both experiences.

I, for one, was baptized a month after I was born, but though sent to Catholic grade school and high school, I managed to graduate from both without much of a clue regarding the truths of the Catholic Faith. I had grown up loving the Blessed Virgin Mary as my Mother, for instance, but it was only when I went to an authentically Catholic college that I discovered what it is that makes Mary so special and what it is that elevates the Church (of which she is the exemplar) above all other churches.

Having had this experience of being both a cradle Catholic and a kind of convert to my own religion, I'm thrilled to hand on to you in the following pages not only what I have received but also what I have looked up, what I have discovered after some embarrassingly ignorant and occasionally awkward moments, and what I have learned through more than fifty years of Catholic living, thirty-five of which have been very intentional.

You might wonder why.

Why, I mean, should I write this book, and why should you read it rather than simply look up this stuff yourself? No doubt you have the wisdom of the Internet at your fingertips—but, in fact, that's precisely why I have written this book. Much as I appreciate the wide-ranging and often quite accurate information available from the screens at my disposal, there is more to what every Catholic should know than what you will find even in the *Catechism of the Catholic Church*, let alone on Wikipedia.

Whether you are a Cradle Catholic, Convert, or Curious Inquirer, when reviewing *What Every Catholic Should Know*, you will quickly find there are more Catholic customs, traditions, habits, and points of etiquette than there are articles of the Creed. So, for easier access, my bet is that you will find it handy to have all this lore in one fifty-thousand-word document, divided into chapters, preprinted, and bound—you know, in a book.

Historically, books of what every Catholic should know are called catechisms, named for the question-and-answer method and including a traditional fourfold progression of *The Creed* (What Catholics Believe), *The Commandments* (What Catholics Do, often thought of as What Catholics Don't Do, but frequently supplemented by the Beatitudes to lend a positive, New Testament, can-do note), and *The Sacraments* and *Prayer* (a two-part answer to the question, How in the world can Catholics live this way?).

Since Pope St. John Paul II gave us, among his many other gifts, a universal catechism called, fittingly, *Catechism of the Catholic Church*, we don't need to worry about providing in this slim volume the entire panoply of Catholic beliefs.

In addition to the *Catechism*, I recommend to readers the new *Code of Canon Law* (promulgated, again by John Paul II, in 1983) as a very handy reference book for what Catholics can and can't do.

These two important books, along with the Holy Bible, will give you more than a lifetime's worth of material to study in order to know what Catholics believe and do. Here in this book, then, we won't duplicate all you will find there, but rather focus on those Catholic customs, traditions, and practices that are in danger of being forgotten but that have been, for centuries, the joy of Catholics to remember.

Take the Catholics in Japan around the mid-nineteenth century. They had been living underground—no, not literally, but they had to hide the practice of their Catholic Faith—for nearly two hundred years, since Christianity had been banned along with all foreigners in 1638. That was only ninety years after St. Francis Xavier had brought the Gospel to Japan and, with his fellow early Jesuits and the missionaries who followed, succeeded in building up the flock to three hundred thousand—enough to prompt persecution, martyrdom, and the general prohibition of Christianity.

Did the Japanese Catholics lose their faith? Did the Church in Japan die? No one in the West knew because missionary priests who tried to enter the country from 1638 to 1853 (when Japan was finally reopened to the West) did not live to tell about what they found in Japan. They, too, were martyred.

The answers came on March 17, 1865. That was the day Fr. Bernard Petitjean, priest of the Paris Foreign Mission Society, while standing near the altar in the beautiful, newly built Oura Church in Nagasaki, was tapped on the shoulder by a Japanese woman. When he turned, she greeted him saying, "We have the same heart as you."

"We" were the hidden Japanese Catholics, the Kirishitan, whom she represented. These Kirishitan (from the Portuguese *cristao*) had been watching the priests, wondering if they were the successors to the ancient Fathers who had brought the Faith to Japan centuries before. The Japanese Catholics had a litmus test: Were the priests in communion with the pontiff in Rome? Did they honor the image of the Virgin Mary? Did they live in celibacy?

A small group had approached Fr. Petitjean as he made his rounds of the city in his priestly garb, hoping as he did so to attract interested Japanese. He took them to the church to tell them something of the Faith. He made an act of reverence at the main altar after they had entered the church, and that's when he received the tap on the shoulder. Imagine his surprise at the woman's news.

"We have the same heart as you."

On behalf of the group, she asked insistently to see St. Mariasama. When Fr. Petitjean showed her the altar of Our Lady, the woman saw the infant Jesus in His mother's arms and said it was Jesussama. She then told the priest there were thirteen hundred underground Catholics in the area and they had retained the customs from the ancient Fathers. "A few days ago, we entered the sad season." (This was Lent.) "We celebrate the birth of Jesussama on the twenty-fifth of the cold month."

They had not had the Eucharist for more than two hundred years, for they had not had a priest during those two long centuries. But they had kept the rite of Baptism, they had kept the seasons of the liturgical year, and they had kept their Savior's mother as their own according to His words from the Cross: "Behold your mother."

The woman was a midwife named Elizabeth Tsuru—they had kept the custom of Christian names. They had lived in persecution and isolation, receiving and passing on the religion and faith of their forebears since the time of St. Francis Xavier's mission in 1549.

From 1549 to 1865 to the twenty-first century in which we find ourselves now, what every Catholic should know has been passed on. Let's start with what the great St. Francis Xavier taught the Japanese, what they held so firmly and passed along so faithfully. He used to enter a town and ring his bell to attract the children. He'd teach them the basics of the Faith in songs, and the happy children would bring their joyful music home, thus becoming little missionaries in their own right, sharing the Gospel with their families.

We won't be using bells and songs in this book, but the joy of children in their newfound faith will accompany us, as will the prayers of the martyrs.

With Elizabeth Tsuru, we will enter the church building and see what we find there. With her fellow Kirishitan, we will take a look at Mary and the Communion of Saints. We will travel through the seasons of the liturgical year, from the birth of Jesus through the sad season to His Resurrection. And lastly, we will consider the papacy He left us and the priesthood He instituted, as well as the other vocations to which God invites His children.

Do you know everything a Catholic should know? Like the hidden Christians of Japan, we find ourselves in strange and often unfriendly times. There may be some customs we have let fall along the way, but there's no time like the present to reacquaint ourselves with our heritage, our patrimony, our treasures.

After using just a few loaves and fishes to feed thousands, Jesus commanded His disciples, "Gather up the leftover fragments, that nothing may be lost" (John 6:12).

The missionaries, the martyrs, the holy priests, and the families who have gone before us—the entire Communion of Saints—couldn't exhaust the generosity of Christ and the nourishment He provides. They have been waiting for us, praying for us to delight in what they have carefully guarded and rejoice to hand down to us.

We, too, are in a position to gather up the fragments so that nothing may be lost. Come along, then, and see if you don't find, among the fragments that follow, food for your hungry soul and refreshment for your spiritual life. Whether we are called to be martyrs, underground Catholics, or merely witnesses in the modern age, there is no shortage of food for the journey. Turn the page and let the feast begin.

Chapter 1

In and around the Church

A Catholic is a person who has plucked up courage to face the incredible and inconceivable idea that something else may be wiser than he is.

—G. K. Chesterton

Recently I had the honor of being godmother for a new convert from Nepal. On the morning of the day he was scheduled to enter the Church—that afternoon he would be baptized, confirmed, and receive his first Holy Communion—we met at my parish for a holy hour: that is, an hour spent before the Real Presence of Jesus in the Holy Eucharist exposed on the altar.

We had planned to meet outside the church building, but, as always, I was late. This prompted a text from my prospective godson: "I am in the church."

I laughed, thinking, *I'm not that late! Did I miss the whole thing?*

He meant he had entered the church building, and I was happy he had not waited for me. Why stand outside when there's a warm welcome waiting within? And yet I loved the double meaning of his text: nothing like entering a church in preparation for entering the Church.

We begin, then, with a distinction.

"The Church" with a capital *C* refers to the one, holy, catholic, apostolic Church founded by Our Lord Jesus Christ to perpetuate His presence among us and to leave us a clear guide and guardian of the Truth of the Faith.

"The church" with a small *c* refers to the church building wherein Jesus' Body, Blood, Soul, and Divinity in the consecrated little white host (the Holy Eucharist) dwells in the tabernacle. It's the building where the Holy Sacrifice of the Mass takes place upon the altar. It is true that "churches" with that first small *c* can also refer to religious institutions (and their places of worship) other than the Catholic Church, but in this book we will be using "church" with a small *c* to refer primarily to a Catholic house of God.

Similarly, "Faith" with a capital *F* refers to the deposit of the Faith left by Jesus in the custody of the Church, whereas "faith" with a small *f* refers to any individual's share in that revealed truth, as well as referring to many other sorts of belief. Hence my prospective godson had faith that I would arrive though I was late, but more importantly he was soon to receive the gift of faith (the theological virtue) at his Baptism when he proclaimed his willingness to accept the fullness of the Faith (of the Church).

And finally, while on the subject of capital and small letters, let me explain why you will see quite a few capital *H*s in this book.

When I was young, it was a common custom to capitalize pronouns referring to God, as a sign of reverence. When I got older, I found such capitalization in most of the devotional books that I read, again as a sign of reverence for the One without whom none of us would be here to capitalize or, alternatively, leave first letters small. And thus it was with a shock that I found, as I got even older, that the *H*s in "He," "His," and "Him" (and so on) in reference to God were being dropped, and this seemed to me a horrible sign of irreverence.

Imagine my second shock when, researching for this book, I discovered that the devotional practice of capitalizing pronouns referring to God is actually a relatively recent custom. If it has declined in the last thirty years, that is a declension from a pious practice of maybe only one hundred years before that. That leaves something like eighteen centuries, since the time of Christ, during which the most devout of writers—such as the authors of the New Testament, the translators of the Holy Scripture, and the Fathers and Doctors of the Church—did not capitalize in this way.

I choose to continue this relatively recent devotional practice, and even hope to convert others to the usage, because I find it helpful, especially in our God-hostile times, for keeping up my courage and my reverence, as well as for counteracting the pervasive abuse of God's holy name. Finally, I find such capitalization consistently helpful for clarity. "When God told Moses to take off his shoes, he knew he would" is just a tad easier to understand when written, "When God told Moses to take off his shoes, He knew he would."

Nonetheless, you should know, as I found out, that when another Catholic author does not employ such capitalization, no disrespect is meant, and the author is holding to an even older tradition than I am.

If this seems like too many distinctions, just remember what happened to the man I know who thought LOL meant "Lots of Love" rather than "Laughing Out Loud." However important the advice he texted to his college-aged children, he always concluded with LOL, thus accidentally ensuring they never took him too seriously!

We can conclude in illustration of our first and most important distinction (between "Church" and "church") that while laughter in the Church (the Mystical Body of Christ) is always a welcome sign of the joy of the saints, laughter in the church (building) is usually frowned upon, due to its tendency to distract and disrupt the prayer of others.

What, then, if not laughter, do we find upon entering the church?

Among the greatest gifts that Jesus left us are the seven sacraments, and in the church we find all that is needed for the conferring of these gifts.

The seven sacraments are Baptism, Confession (also called Penance or Reconciliation), the Eucharist, Confirmation, Marriage, Holy Orders (the Priesthood), and the Anointing of the Sick (formerly called Extreme Unction, so named for its use as a last anointing for the dying).

With the exception of the Anointing of the Sick, the sacraments of the Church are ordinarily experienced in the church. So on entering any Catholic church, one typically sees or can find upon looking the following items: a baptismal font; a confessional (or reconciliation room); the altar where transubstantiation—the change of substance of bread and wine into the Body, Blood, Soul, and Divinity of Jesus—takes place during Mass; and the tabernacle where the hidden Jesus abides (the consecrated hosts left unconsumed after Mass) with, nearby, a flickering red candle (often suspended from the ceiling), which is the sanctuary lamp indicating Jesus is truly present.

The baptismal font may be a permanent fixture in the front or back of the church, or it may be movable.

Traditional "box style" confessionals are usually in the back of the church by the main entrance (as are reconciliation rooms), or they may be in the transept (in churches designed like a cross, the transepts are the sides of the crossbar).

The altar is front and center, fittingly, as it is the main focus of attention during the Holy Sacrifice of the Mass. The area around the altar is called the sanctuary and is off limits for all but those specially sanctioned to be there; think priests, deacons, altar servers, sacristans (who take care of the paten or little plate on which the priest's host rests during Mass, the ciborium in which are the other consecrated hosts, the chalice, the altar linens, etc.), and others with similar responsibility.

In older churches an altar rail clearly marks off the sacred area of the sanctuary, but even in churches without altar rails, there is usually a step separating the sanctuary from the rest of the church. The important thing to know is that while the whole church is a holy place, the sanctuary especially is holy ground. We can think of Jesus in the Blessed Sacrament (the Eucharist) in the sanctuary—on the altar and in the tabernacle—as the fulfillment of the burning bush that prefigured Him, on fire with love and yet not consumed. God told Moses, "Do not come near; take your sandals off your feet, for the place on which you are standing is holy ground." After God's self-revelation "Moses hid his face, for he was afraid to look at God" (Exodus 3:5–6).

We are certainly not forbidden to look at Jesus in the Blessed Sacrament. We are invited and encouraged to look upon Him hidden in the little white host when this accidental form of bread remains after the consecration and Jesus is truly there: both when the priest elevates the host during Mass and outside of Mass when the Blessed Sacrament is exposed in the gold monstrance (which often looks like a sunburst) on the altar for our adoration. But this is God, and, remembering our place as mere creatures, we must honor the sacred space of the sanctuary by keeping the distance the Church, our Mother, has set for us.

This is why, in the sacraments of Baptism and Holy Matrimony, it is a great honor for the recipients to be allowed very near or sometimes in the sanctuary itself.

The tabernacle may be behind the altar or to one side of it, though occasionally in larger churches the tabernacle is kept in a separate room. Look for the red lamplight, and when you have found it, you will have found Jesus! You can visit with

Him there, kneeling or sitting in a pew as close as you can get to Him, and chatting with Him about everything.

Still, as St. Thérèse of the Child Jesus used to say, "It is not to remain in a golden ciborium that He comes to us each day from heaven; it's to find another heaven, infinitely more dear to Him than the first: the heaven of our soul, made to His image, the living temple of the adorable Trinity!"[1] The church is, then, the place where you will also find—every day of the year but one, and in many churches more than once a day, and on Sundays sometimes several times—the Holy Sacrifice of the Mass taking place, the priest in the person of Jesus offering the Sacrifice of Calvary, by the power of the Holy Spirit, to the Heavenly Father. The one day there is no complete Mass is Good Friday. Since it is the very day of Jesus' sacrifice of Himself on Calvary, there is no Mass in Catholic churches but rather a liturgy in which the faithful come together to hear the Gospel account of His Passion, venerate an image of the holy Cross on which He died, and receive Holy Communion to be united with Him. Then on Holy Saturday, there is silence—until the Easter Vigil. And yet, it is absolutely true to say that first and foremost the church is the place for the Holy Sacrifice of the Mass and for Jesus' Real Presence dwelling among us.

Let's go into the church, then, entering by the main front door.

---

1   St. Thérèse of Lisieux, *Story of a Soul*, trans. John Clarke, O.C.D. (Washington, DC: ICS Publications), 104.

Chapter 2

Making a Visit

Let us throw ourselves into the ocean of His goodness, where every failing will be canceled and anxiety turned into love.

—St. Paul of the Cross

We have entered a Catholic church. To our left and right, on each side of the door, are holy water fonts. This is the first of many sacramentals we will find.

The *sacraments* are the seven necessary channels of grace (Christ's life in us), signs effecting what they signify, instituted by Our Lord during His lifetime on earth and entrusted to the Church for our salvation. The *sacramentals* are in number practically uncountable, given to us by Holy Mother Church as incidental (as contrasted with essential) conduits of grace.

What are the big moments in our lives? For each of these, there is a sacrament, so that we may have the grace of Christ, the very life of the Trinity, poured out upon us and into us, strengthening us, nourishing us, drawing us forward into God's arms and saving our souls.

We are born—the Church offers us Baptism, and the sooner the better, since this sacrament erases Original Sin from the soul and grafts the baptized into Christ, the true Vine, making the recipient a member of the Mystical Body and the Communion of Saints.

We get ourselves dirty and need to wash—the Church has a remedy for our soul's stains, washing us clean through Confession. And if, in the worst-case scenario, we cut ourselves off from God through serious sin, Confession not only cleanses our souls of mortal (or deathly) sin but also reconciles us with the Father, who is always welcoming and yearning for our return.

We need sustenance to grow and develop physically, and we need companionship—the Church provides Christ Himself as the food of our souls in the Holy Eucharist, that we may grow and develop spiritually, and He offers Himself as our best friend, ever available and nearer to us than any earthly friend could be.

We get married—the Church is there, allowing us to marry in Christ, with grace for the asking every day, every moment of our married lives until death do us part. Unlike the sacraments that we receive once and which have done their work in us (Baptism and Confirmation), and also unlike the sacraments that we receive frequently so that we may be given again and again their gifts of cleansing, reconciliation, nourishment, and union with Christ, the Sacrament of Holy Matrimony (similar in this way to Holy Orders) is a gift that keeps on giving—we receive it once and it is a continual channel of grace for us.

We fall ill—Holy Mother Church is near us, ready to dispense more grace in the Sacrament of the Anointing of the Sick, that we may be restored to health or strengthened on our way from this life to its fulfillment in the next. This anointing is so powerful that it wipes away all sin and all punishment due to sin. Could there be any better preparation for a straight shot to heaven? Like in Confession, the mercy of Christ is poured out in abundance in this sacrament, because His Death was not in vain but for the very purpose of washing away our sins and bringing us into eternal life with Him.

And yet, as a loving Mother, the Church is not satisfied with only these seven opportunities to care for us. Hence, the sacramentals. We enter the church and there is the holy water, except in the Sacred Triduum: the days of Jesus' Last Supper and Agony in the Garden on Holy Thursday, His Passion and Death on the Cross for us on Good Friday, and His time in the tomb and descent to free those chained in death on Holy Saturday. On these days, there is no holy water in the fonts inside the church doors because there is also no Jesus hiding in the tabernacle. The Church hides Him further away, covers His images (and those of His friends) in purple cloth for mourning, and bids us wait for the cleansing water of Easter.

Normally, however, where we enter there is holy water. Why? Our first action on entering the church is to bless ourselves in the name of the Father, the Son, and the Holy Spirit. Our prayer within this holy house of God is thus sanctified from the first moment, as our day is sanctified from the first moment with our morning offering.

The morning offering is a prayer that leads into the day, allowing us to offer all of it—our joys, sorrows, thoughts, feelings, words, and actions—to God in union with Christ and His sacrifice. Since it is in union with Him that our own actions are sanctified, we offer them, through the Immaculate Heart of Mary, in union with the Holy Sacrifice of the Mass throughout the world. Everything we have is from Him, everything we can do is by His mercy, and we offer it all back to Him for the salvation of the world. (You will find the morning offering and other prayers in the last chapter of this book.)

Similarly, blessing ourselves with holy water leads us into our time in church, and when we use this sanctified water with reverence, the Church gives our souls a little bath: we are cleansed of venial sin, and our prayer in the church is all the more joyful for us and for God.

Okay, we're in. What's next?

If you can, locate the tabernacle. Remember, if you see the red sanctuary lamp, the Blessed Sacrament (the Eucharist has this special name because it is God Himself) is present, which means Jesus is there. Greet Him. Say hello, thank Him for bringing you into His presence, apologize that it took you so long, complain about the traffic—whatever comes to mind. Yes, He knows it all because He is God, but, yes, too, He loves to hear it from you because His delight is to be with the children of men.

Because Jesus is waiting in the tabernacle constantly, because He longs for our company and is there ready to bestow every blessing, our visiting Him at church is a great idea, even at times when Mass is not offered.

So you have come for a visit. You have entered, blessed yourself, said hello. Now find a place to get comfortable in His presence. You stand beside a pew and, unless it is Good Friday or Holy Saturday when He is not in the tabernacle (and so you simply bow to the altar), genuflect before entering the pew. This is our sign of reverence, acknowledgment of who He is and who we are. Facing the front of the church and standing beside the entrance to the pew, kneel on your right knee, and with your right hand again make the Sign of the Cross, tracing it from your forehead to your chest, then from your left shoulder to your right.

The genuflection entering the pew is only for a moment— you usually do not stay long on that right knee—but if the Blessed Sacrament is exposed on the altar in the monstrance, genuflect on both knees to honor Jesus, true God and true man right before you, though He is hidden under the appearance of bread.

In the pew, you might kneel or sit. Many kneel for their first prayer to Him and then sit. The important thing to know is that you are with the One who loves you most, and there is nothing to worry about, nothing to fear. Just be yourself and pour out your heart to Him.

If you don't know what to say to Our Lord, you can start with prayers you know by heart (or from a book) or simply look at Him and let Him look at you. You are together; that is what matters.

There is a beautiful Catholic practice of not turning around or looking behind you when you are in church. Most likely the tabernacle and certainly the altar are before you: there is where your treasure is, so there, too, is your heart, and where your treasure and your heart are, there your attention will be too. Naturally, if you are in the pew with a prayer book or holy card or spiritual reading, feel free to focus on these as well, but your posture should be forward facing.

Exceptions to this "attention up front" are made when there is a momentous event requiring your attention in the back of the church, such as (1) at a wedding, when all rise and turn to see the bride entering, representing the Church gloriously bedecked to meet Christ, her Spouse; (2) at a funeral, when the casket is escorted in, bearing a Christian who has gone to see God and whose remains are sacred; and (3) if there seems to be a medical emergency in the pew behind yours (including the sound of someone perhaps fainting, but not including boisterous or unhappy children whose equally unhappy parents are with them).

If you are at church, whether for a visit or before or after Mass, and the priest (or another) opens the tabernacle, it is customary to kneel in reverence while the small door is open. The King of kings is within, you may have a glimpse of His humble trappings, and since He is the reason you are there, it makes sense to bow before Him.

Around the walls of the church you will see fourteen Stations of the Cross. Originating with St. Francis of Assisi, these are reminders of the different stages of Christ's Passion and Death. Another wonderful Catholic custom especially appropriate for Fridays (and most of all practiced on Fridays in

Lent, with the entire parish invited to attend) is the "making" of the Way of the Cross. If you are in church for a visit (again, outside of the Holy Sacrifice of the Mass or perhaps making your thanksgiving after Mass), you can accompany Christ spiritually by standing before each of these Stations and praying (with or without a booklet) and reflecting on the event that each of them represents. These Stations are another sacramental.

With luck, you will see beautiful statues at the front or sides or back of the church. These, too, are sacramentals: images of the friends of God, the saints. You might want to leave your pew (genuflecting to the tabernacle as you go) and approach more closely. These statues represent our brothers and sisters who are now perfectly happy with God, and happy to put in a good word for us. They know what we suffer—they have suffered the same, or something like it. Let the statue remind you of this holy one, and open your heart before such a good friend of yours and God's.

If no one else is in the church during your visit, there is nothing wrong with praying aloud, but be conscious that when others are present, your prayers are better said silently (or very, very quietly) so they don't distract your fellow visitors. Silence is also a sign of respect and an opening for God to speak to you in the quiet of your heart.

At the end of your visit with Jesus, when leaving the pew and the church, you do everything you did upon entering, only in opposite order. You can say goodbye and thank You to Jesus, then genuflect just outside the pew (on one knee usually, but on both knees if the Blessed Sacrament is exposed). Before you leave the church, bless yourself with holy water, taking one last loving look at the tabernacle.

It is sad to leave the presence of the living God, but we have duties and commitments outside of church, and we must go. Invite Him, then, to accompany you on your way. "Come with me, Little Jesus!" you might ask as you depart. And then, don't worry; with God's grace you will soon be back. We're going to visit again, in fact, in the very next chapter, to take a closer look at the Holy Sacrifice of the Mass.

Chapter 3

The Mass: Ever Ancient, Ever New

If we really understood the Mass, we would die of joy.

— St. John Vianney

I remember years ago when a friend gave me an example of the devil's spectacular talent for dividing (in his attempt to conquer) upright hearts. My friend was reflecting on the Mass and remarked, "Have you ever noticed that at the very moment Our Lord has designed to most perfectly unite us to one another, when we receive Him in Holy Communion, we can't help but notice whether the person in front of us is bowing or kneeling, receiving on the tongue or in the hand? And who can then help making some sort of judgment?"

My friend's observation highlights the dilemma we find ourselves in today regarding the most perfect gift God has given us to give back to Him—namely, the Holy Sacrifice of the Mass.

When we begin to talk about the Mass, we find ourselves in deep waters, and our consideration (like my friend's experience at Communion) is liable to be divisive for two reasons.

First, because the Holy Sacrifice of the Mass, as Christ's Passion and Death on Calvary, is very profound and mysterious. This explains the deep waters.

Second, because in 1969 a new order of the Mass was introduced and promulgated that, whether this was the plan or not, effectively suppressed the old order of the Mass. Thus the Latin Mass everyone knew disappeared overnight, and it did not make an international comeback until 2007 when Pope Benedict XVI issued a *motu proprio* (an edict from the pope to the Church) clarifying the pastoral situation and re-presenting for universal use the 1962 Missal, which contained the old, or Tridentine, Latin Mass.

In his *motu proprio*, Pope Benedict renamed the old Mass "the Extraordinary Form" and papally endorsed it alongside the Ordinary Form of the Mass that had been introduced after Vatican Council II.

If you are a Catholic, new or old, or interested in Catholic things enough to be reading this book, and you don't know why the sequence of events I've just recounted would cause division (or that it has caused division), God bless you! You have made my day (even imagining your guilelessness has made my day). But in order for you to understand what comes next, I will do my duty and explain.

For those who had grown up with the old Mass—the Mass in Latin with the priest facing the altar (and facing away from the people; *ad orientam*, this is called)—to have the Mass they knew taken away from them so instantaneously and globally was, to say the least, disorienting.

For some it was, no doubt, interesting, exciting, and fun. Some people enjoy change, and others may have found the new order of the Mass required them to pay more attention, which, in itself, is a good thing to do at Mass.

But the sea change this innovation introduced was a cause of pain and sorrow for many, as well as a cause for many other changes, a great number of them unauthorized.

When Pope Benedict XVI brought back the old Mass, this was not merely an effort to satisfy those who missed it. Considering that nearly forty years had passed since the promulgation of the new Mass, we can see that the youngest of those who had grieved over the loss of the old Mass were now at least forty years old, which means that for everyone under forty (and more likely under fifty), the new Mass was pretty much all they had ever known. Not to mention that older generations had been given forty years to get over their loss.

The reality is that Pope Benedict saw the need in the Church, the Mystical Body of Christ and the household of the faithful, for the return of the Tridentine Mass (so called because originally it came from the Council of Trent).

The consequence? For those who did still miss the old Mass (the Extraordinary Form), they had it returned to them. For those who were used to the new Mass, loved it, and felt no need for a change, they still had the new Mass (the Ordinary Form).

But between those two groups, there were and are those who only ever knew the Ordinary Form but were now exposed to the Extraordinary Form and much preferred it. There were also those who had entered the Church by droves (when there's a flood, you want to be in an ark) and discovered that there was now a mystifying choice of Mass options. Many of these new Catholics have, as my husband and I have been noticing recently with young converts we meet, a fascination with the beauty and mystery of the Extraordinary Form.

Among those cradle Catholics and converts alike who are discovering with joy the Tridentine Mass, their newfound love of the old Mass raises the question, What in the world was the Church thinking to set it aside for forty years?

On the other hand, for those who have known and loved the *new* Mass, those who feel no need for (and often some suspicion of) this new old Mass, the question is, What in the world was the Church thinking to bring back another form of the Mass when we were fine with what she's given us these past forty years?

What every Catholic (and every non-Catholic, for that matter) needs to know is that the Church is our Mother, she loves us and teaches us, and she is allowed to give us (as every mother worth her salt does) more good things than we can possibly fully enjoy.

My husband and I once had a great teacher who defined heaven as "every good thing, all at once, forever." Meanwhile, we have many, many good things that we are able to enjoy, but not all together during the limited time of our exile here in this life.

I grew up with the Ordinary Form of the Mass. When the Extraordinary Form started making a comeback (in the mid-1980s when Pope St. John Paul II allowed its local use to be determined by each bishop), I went once and was not enthralled.

After Pope Benedict's universal permission for the use of the 1962 Missal, I had friends who very happily attended the Extraordinary Form every day. One of these friends was a saintly man who died, and at his funeral I read in the program that he had requested the Extraordinary Form Requiem Mass so that all who attended could be introduced to the beauty and simplicity of the old Mass.

I was moved. My friend wanted to share this gift with me, so I tried to receive it worthily. I bought a missal for the old Mass, and I discovered that the reason I had felt so left out the few times I had previously attended the Extraordinary Form is that you really, really need a missal to follow closely what is going on (for some, until you get the idea; for someone like me, probably forever). I fell in love with the Extraordinary Form, but I prayed to Mary, our Mother and exemplar of the Church, "Please let me love both forms of the Mass, since you have given us both, and I know you only give good and wonderful gifts."

She answered my prayer, and I do love both forms of the Mass, though sometimes I prefer one over the other, and then my preference reverses itself and I prefer the other over the one. My defense? Both are from Holy Mother Church, both are good, and, as Pope Benedict clearly stated, both are equally the Holy Sacrifice of the Mass.

What we need to know about the Mass theologically—and this applies, equally, to both forms—is articulated in the following passage:

> At the Last Supper, on the night when He was betrayed, Our Saviour instituted the eucharistic sacrifice of His Body and Blood. He did this in order to perpetuate the sacrifice of the Cross throughout the centuries until He should come again, and so to entrust to His beloved spouse, the Church, a memorial of His death and resurrection: a sacrament of love, a sign of unity, a bond of charity, a paschal banquet in which Christ is eaten, the mind is filled with grace, and a pledge of future glory is given to us.

Who wrote these lovely and true words? It was a group effort—a combination of the words of the Fathers of Vatican II, St. Augustine, and St. Thomas Aquinas. This is paragraph 47 from *Sacrosanctum Concilium* (the Constitution on the Sacred Liturgy), and it leads us to the important point that the actual documents of Vatican Council II are a good place to start when delving into what every Catholic living in our day should know.

By providing a quotation from our most recent ecumenical council, I hope to whet your appetite for more. Like those holy and faithful ones of Japan, we are not surrounded by a friendly and instructive culture. Nonetheless, like the saints and martyrs before us, we can find plentiful sustenance in our churches and more instruction than we will have time

to absorb from the sources of truth that are the Magisterium
(teaching office of the Church) and Tradition.

What shall we say, then, about the Mass?

Let's go back into the church building, settle into a pew,
and attend to the Holy Sacrifice.

Chapter 4

How to Go to Mass

If you find it impossible to pray, hide behind your good angel and charge him to pray in your stead.

— St. John Vianney

When we enter the church for the Holy Sacrifice of the Mass and bless ourselves with the holy water, we've begun our ablutions. Holy Mother Church wants us to be as clean as possible for this big event, so the beginning of the Mass (in both forms) is about silently confessing our sins and receiving God's outpouring of mercy.

Next, the Church becomes our teacher, sharing with us the Word of God. In the Extraordinary Form, there is a non-Gospel Scripture reading, and then the Gospel. In the Ordinary Form, we hear two non-Gospel readings on weekdays (one of them a psalm with responses), and then the Gospel; on Sundays and solemnities, we hear three non-Gospel readings (an Old Testament and New Testament reading, as well as the psalm), followed by the Gospel.

A professor I once had, a holy priest, used to ask the question, "How does the Church read the Bible?" and then answer, "The Church reads the Bible as Liturgy."

"Liturgy" refers to the common prayer of the Church, and it includes both the Liturgy of the Mass and the Liturgy of the

Hours, which is also called the Divine Office and sometimes referred to as "praying the Breviary" (the Breviary being the book containing these prayers).

Within the Divine Office—which all priests and many religious are bound to say and laypeople are invited to say too—over a four-week cycle the Church prays the entirety of the Psalter, the 150 psalms from the Bible. Special feasts have proper prayers and psalms and canticles (songs from the Old and New Testaments), and there is an education to be had here beyond anything imaginable. Which psalms, readings, canticles, and antiphons the Church has chosen for various feasts and saints is no accident but, in fact, how the Church reads the Bible.

The same is true for the Mass. The proper prayers (and the common prayers, for that matter) of the old Mass, along with the longer readings, contain an excess of riches, but then so do the Scriptures chosen for the liturgical cycle of the new Mass.

After the readings, there is a homily or sermon. A homily is an explanation of the Scriptures that have just been read. A sermon, on the other hand, is an instruction on any topic the priest deems helpful for the congregation's spiritual edification. After Vatican Council II, priests were asked to give homilies at Mass, though they can occasionally give sermons as well.

After the homily, if it is a Sunday or a high feast, comes the Creed. This is the foundation of what every Catholic should know, as well as the pinnacle of our Faith. The word "creed" comes from *credo*, Latin for "I believe," but there is another name for the creed: the *symbol* of our Faith. The *Catechism of the Catholic Church* explains:

The Greek word *symbolon* meant half of a broken object, for example, a seal presented as a token of recognition. The broken parts were placed together to verify the bearer's identity. The symbol of faith, then, is a sign of recognition and communion between believers. *Symbolon* also means a gathering, collection, or summary. A symbol of faith is a summary of the principal truths of the faith. (*CCC*, 188)

There are many authentic Catholic creeds because there are many true summaries of the principal truths of our Faith, but the two most familiar (because most commonly used) are (1) the Apostles' Creed and (2) the Niceno-Constantinopolitan Creed. The Apostles' Creed is "the Creed of the Roman Church, the See of Peter, the first of the Apostles, to which he brought the common faith," as St. Ambrose said.[1] The shorter of the two, it is said at the beginning of the Rosary. The Niceno-Constantinopolitan Creed is so named from the first two Ecumenical Councils of 325 and 381, but it's called more simply the Nicene Creed. It contains a more explicit and fuller summary of what the faithful believes, and it is said at Mass.

Because we say the Nicene Creed each Sunday, it can become a routine formula, but it is much more than that. We forget the power and grace this ancient prayer holds. As St. Ambrose tells us, "The Creed is the spiritual seal, our heart's meditation and an ever-present guardian; it is, unquestionably, the treasure of our soul."[2]

After the Creed comes the Offertory, when the priest offers to God the bread and wine that will become the Body and Blood of Christ. This is our opportunity to join with Christ and offer ourselves. Place yourself on the paten as the priest holds up the bread—offer everything you have and are to God, to be used by Him however He wills.

There is a tremendous moment in the Offertory when the priest adds one drop of water to the chalice of wine. Just as

---

1   St. Ambrose, *Explanatio symboli* 7, quoted in *CCC*, 194.
2   Ibid., 1, quoted in *CCC*, 197.

the drop of water becomes intermingled and indistinguishable from the wine, so we pray here to become entirely one with Christ.

And then comes the holiest part of the Mass: the Roman Canon, as it is called in the Extraordinary Form, or Eucharistic Prayer in the Ordinary Form. Now we are truly entering the mysteries; and silence with focused attention—in short, the utmost reverence—is called for.

At the heart of the Mass, the unbloody sacrifice of Christ on the Cross, is the moment of transubstantiation. This is the moment of the consecration when the priest, in the person of Christ, says with Him the words that change the very substance of the bread and wine into the Body, Blood, Soul, and Divinity of Jesus. Each particle of bread and each droplet of wine contains the whole Christ, and yet both elements of bread and wine are there to symbolize the separation of His Body from His Blood at death.

The accidents of bread and wine—their taste, smell, texture, and shape—remain the same, and perhaps the greater miracle is that these accidents subsist (continue to exist) when what is before us has been changed and is truly now Christ, Our Lord. He knew that it would have been too much, too strange, too unfitting for us to eat Him in His appearance (His reality with the proper accidents) as man, and so He found a way to give us Himself under these accidental forms that we normally eat and drink. What love and what a mystery!

Hence the priest's proclamation, "The Mystery of Faith," followed by our response. The Mystery of Faith, truly, is the Blessed Sacrament that has just been confected at his words, the sacrament that, of them all, is holiest because it is Christ Himself.

I have a Catholic cousin who explained to his non-Catholic fiancée this Mystery of Faith—Jesus' Real Presence in the

Blessed Sacrament. She laughed and flatly refused to believe this was what he believed. When he insisted he believed it, she argued she had proof he did not.

"If you really believed that, why do you only go to Mass on Sunday? You don't even visit the church during the week!"

My cousin humbly admitted her point—not that he didn't believe this doctrine but that his life (though he went to Mass dutifully every Sunday) certainly did not reflect his belief very effectively. From then on, he went to Mass almost every day and tried not to pass a church without making a visit to Jesus hiding in the tabernacle inside, and she in turn came to believe and converted to the Faith. This is the Mystery of Faith in action, generating a fitting degree of awe and gratitude.

After the consecration and its accompanying prayers, the Our Father is prayed. And then, soon after, the priest makes his Communion and we are invited—after admission of our unworthiness and our prayer that Christ will, with a word, prepare our hearts properly—to Holy Communion as well.

The conditions for receiving Holy Communion used to be widely known. When my mother and father were dating, she (a cradle Catholic from Detroit) had somehow got the impression that he (from the Middle East) was Jewish. But when they attended Mass together and he went up to receive Communion, she knew he was Catholic. In the late 1950s, no one would have dared receive unless properly disposed—even non-Catholics knew that!

To be properly disposed to receive Holy Communion, one must (1) be a baptized Catholic; (2) be in the state of grace—that is, having committed no mortal sin or having received absolution from the priest after confessing the mortal sin(s); and (3) have fasted for an hour from food and drink (water and medicine are allowed) before receiving the Eucharist.

If you are at Mass and are not disposed or ready to receive, it is customary, if so desired, to approach the priest with arms crossed over your chest in an *X* (fingers on the opposite shoulders) for a blessing.

If you are ready and disposed to receive Holy Communion, ask your guardian angel to help you receive Him with the utmost adoration, love, and reverence.

Because the consecrated host we receive is truly Christ and because every tiniest particle of this host contains the entirety of the Incarnate God, the best way of receiving the Holy Eucharist is on the tongue so that there is less danger of any particle being accidentally lost or inadvertently dropped. This is God we are receiving, and our reverence and care in receiving Him is an integral part of our adoration.

You may be in a church where there is an altar rail used. Once you are kneeling there, you will wait for the priest to approach you. When he is before you, if you are at Mass in the Extraordinary Form, the priest will say, "Corpus Domini Nostri Jesu Christi custodiat animam tuam in vitam aeternam. Amen." This means, "May the Body of Our Lord, Jesus Christ, preserve your soul unto life everlasting." Because the priest says, "Amen," there is no need to repeat this as you await reception of the Sacrament. Your job is simply to open your mouth and put your tongue forward so that the priest can place the host there.

If you are kneeling at the altar rail at Mass in the Ordinary Form, the priest will say, as he holds the host before you, either, "Corpus Christi" or "The Body of Christ." You respond, "Amen," which means, "So be it," your acknowledgment of belief and agreement, like a tiny, last-minute creed. Open your mouth and put your tongue forward. Once the priest has placed the Blessed Sacrament in your mouth, make the Sign of the Cross and return to your pew.

If the church does not have or use the communion rail, you approach the priest, deacon, or extraordinary minister of Holy Communion in a line of communicants, and in this case you have an opportunity to show special reverence for Our Lord when you are second in line. As the person ahead of you receives, you can bow or genuflect to show your adoration and help prepare yourself to welcome Jesus.

When it is your turn to receive, after hearing "Corpus Christi" or "The Body of Christ," first respond, "Amen," then open your mouth and put your tongue forward. I recommend keeping your hands folded in a prayerful attitude low on your body to indicate to the priest, deacon, or extraordinary minister of Holy Communion that you are about to receive in the mouth rather than the hand. After the consecrated host is placed on your tongue, make the Sign of the Cross; then return to your pew.

You do not genuflect when you are entering the pew after Communion. Think of it this way: genuflection is a sign of reverence to Jesus in the tabernacle, but now you are Jesus' tabernacle. Enter your pew and kneel, and then it is time for your thanksgiving.

How much you have to thank Him for! You can start with His Real Presence in you at this moment and go from there. Or you can ask Him for all that you need, present to Him the people and situations that have been distracting you, or ask Him to help those who have commended themselves to your prayers. You will never in this life be closer to God than you are this minute. Pour out your heart to Him.

The best advice I can give regarding your thanksgiving (and this comes from the great Doctor of Prayer, St. Teresa of Jesus of Avila) is to *close your eyes*. No, not right now, but when you are trying to pray, and especially when you are back in your pew after receiving Jesus and are ready to converse with Him.

We depend so much on our senses that it is hard to shut them off, but at this moment you are with the Creator of the universe. He has done this huge thing of making Himself tiny so that He can be as closely united to you as possible. You have God within you, but meanwhile you may be hearing music or the shuffling of feet (all the others going to and from Communion), possibly smelling the perfume of the woman in front of you, maybe feeling hot or cold or hungry. Close your eyes, and this will give you one less source of distraction. You are with Jesus, your best friend, the Spouse of your soul.

Imagine you have been granted an audience with the person you most admire. Wouldn't you put your cell phone in the other room or ignore it if it beeped? (Though we didn't mention this earlier, it is basic etiquette and a necessity to turn off your phone before you go into church.) Closing your eyes is like turning off your phone. You are free to focus on the One who loves you most; you are free to love Him back, at least for a few minutes, however poorly. Don't worry: Jesus is very interested in everything that interests you, and He has plenty to say in return.

Whole books have been written about Jesus in the Blessed Sacrament, and two especially great ones are *Holy Communion* (by St. Peter Julian Eymard) and *The Holy Eucharist* (by St. Alphonsus de Liguori). Reading such books can help you to receive Our Lord with more attention, love, and joy, though try not to worry if distractions are the language of your prayer. Again, closing your eyes will help, and don't worry about your poverty: He has brought you all riches in bringing you Himself.

When Mass is over, remain standing until the priest and his retinue have processed out of the church. If there is a hymn being sung, it is proper to remain standing until the last verse is completed, whether or not you are singing too. If you are not singing, you might want to close your eyes and continue your prayer. And then? Then you are ready to revive two truly valuable customs that will honor God and provide you with a final grace.

First, refrain from talking to those around you until outside the church building. You are in the presence of God (remember that sanctuary lamp!) and have God within you, and you are also in a house of prayer. Out of respect for those who may still be praying and out of respect for the angels who will continue praying after you leave, silence is ideal.

The second practice is to kneel down again (or sit, as you prefer) to say some final prayer before you leave church. It may be another week before you are able to pray in this special place again—make the most of it while you can. It may be twenty-four hours, in which case you are a lucky duck, and you will want to thank God for this grace among others.

The traditional understanding is that Jesus' Real Presence remains within you as long as the consecrated host perdures (until it is entirely dissolved), which is about fifteen minutes. This time may not yet have elapsed when Mass is ended, and so you might stay longer with Him who is staying with you.

Sometimes circumstances do not permit your staying long to pray after Mass. If this is true for you—maybe you have a child with you who was ready to go long before Mass was over—you can kneel for a brief prayer to thank Him once again and ask Him to come with you as you leave.

Genuflect outside the pew, and avail yourself of one last blessing with the holy water as you leave the church and one last goodbye to Our Lord in the tabernacle. He loves you more than you will ever know—and He has given you the Mass to show you a glimpse of how much.

Chapter 5

Baptism, Confession, and the Precepts of the Church

Baptism is ransom, forgiveness of debts, death of sin, regeneration of the soul, a resplendent garment, an unbreakable seal, a chariot to heaven, a royal protector, a gift of adoption.

— St. Basil the Great

When we are baptized, we lose something and gain something: Original Sin is wiped from our souls, and God's life is poured in. We become infused with the theological virtues of faith, hope, and charity as the water is poured over our heads and the minister's words, "I baptize you in the name of the Father, and of the Son, and of the Holy Spirit," claim us as God's children.

Those who have been baptized with water and these words are once and for all baptized. This is why when a non-Catholic Christian becomes Catholic—say, at the Easter Vigil—the rite includes Confirmation but no Baptism. If there is uncertainty about whether a previous Baptism used the proper formula (in the name of the Persons of the Holy Trinity), the priest can perform a conditional Baptism (a "just in case" Baptism), but in those cases, God and the angels alone know if it was needed or just an extra little bath.

As a holy priest said to a woman who claimed she had lost her faith, "You can't lose your faith, or I would have to

37

rebaptize you!" But on the other hand, we can kick God out of our souls by rejecting Him when we choose to sin mortally. We are all mortal. That means we all die—our souls and physical bodies part ways at some point in time, which is bodily death.

Is there such a thing as spiritual death? Sadly, there is. It occurs when we know something is seriously wrong (opposed to the Ten Commandments and teachings of the Church in a big way) and we freely choose to do it. Take, for instance, the seventh commandment: thou shalt not steal. If you steal a pack of gum from the store, this is clearly a violation of the seventh commandment. Still, it's a relatively small violation and so a relatively small, or venial, sin. If, however, you get the bright idea to rob a bank, and unhappily none of your fellows talk you out of it, when you attempt to rob that bank you are committing a mortal sin. This is serious stuff, robbing banks, and hence serious sin.

Let's say you get out of the bank with the money, but the police siren is wailing right behind you as you drive away. You could have a moment of remorse due to your fear of jail time and decide to turn yourself in, in hopes of a reduced sentence. Or you might have a moment of enlightenment and turn yourself in because you realize you did wrong and it was a grave injustice to the good people whose money you stole.

The first of these moments of repentance is similar to what we call imperfect contrition. While it's definitely enough to gain you God's forgiveness (if not the state's), you need to go to Confession to set yourself right with God and invite His life (which you have effectively killed in your soul) back to revivify you.

Perfect contrition is like the second type of remorse mentioned—but toward God, it is the realization that your sin is an offense against His perfect goodness, which deserves all your love, which is a far cry from what you gave Him when you committed the mortal sin. In this case, technically you don't have to go to Confession because your perfect contrition has made up for your sin and you have effectively invited God back into your soul.

Did you notice the word "technically" in that last sentence? Actually, if you have committed a mortal sin, get yourself to Confession as soon as possible. It is a pretty dicey game to risk your soul on the question of how perfect your contrition is! The Church teaches us that God's mercy is always available—for any sin whatsoever—in the wonderful Sacrament of Confession. Since Christ Himself gave the Church (through Peter and the Apostles) the promise, "Truly, I say to you, whatever you bind on earth shall be bound in heaven, and whatever you loose on earth shall be loosed in heaven" (Matthew 18:18), we can trust that whatsoever our sins are, they are forgiven in the confessional or reconciliation room (or even outside the bank—where I once got a priest to hear my confession, though I had only been making a simple transaction, not robbing the place).

You can see, then, why this chapter is on Baptism and Confession together. It is through the Sacrament of Baptism that God's life is poured into our souls. It is through sin that we lose it. And it is through the Sacrament of Confession that we can regain His triune presence within us.

When we live in this crazy, upside-down world, the culture of death (as Pope St. John Paul II so aptly named it), we are liable to think that all the madcap adventures people have (you know—living together before marriage, divorcing and remarrying apparently freely, using artificial contraception and sometimes following that up with abortions, getting drunk, smoking or swallowing hallucinogenic drugs, and the list goes on) are simply personal decisions rather than grave offenses against nature and God.

Here is what we need to remember: there is a natural and a supernatural order, and our actions have a bearing upon these orders. God gave us the Church to help us know, even in the midst of contrary cultural norms, the difference between right and wrong, between what pleases Him and what offends Him, and also (not an unimportant point) between what will and will not make us truly happy, in this life and the next.

We have, then, the Ten Commandments, a full list of which is included in the last chapter for easy reference. We have, too, the precepts of the Church, which we list there as well. If, like the rich young man in the Gospel (Mark 10:17), you want to go further than these, we have the evangelical counsels of poverty, chastity, and obedience—you can sell all you have to follow Jesus even more closely, live not only a chaste life (meaning you do not offend against purity but instead live according to the Commandments) but also a celibate life (not getting married and thus not enjoying the gifts that come with that privilege), and even place yourself in obedience to a superior who represents God (say, by entering religious life as a sister, a brother, or a priest).

For most of us, however, it will be enough of a challenge to follow the Ten Commandments and the five precepts of the Church, including getting to Confession at least once a year but ideally more like once a month—or, as I heard it explained from the pulpit recently, if you are struggling with or have struggled with a serious sin, more like once a week.

Since the precepts of the Church are less familiar to most of us than the Commandments (and there are fewer), let's list them here:

1. Attend Mass on Sundays and on holy days of obligation, and rest from servile labor.
2. Confess your sins at least once a year.

3. Receive the Sacrament of the Eucharist at least during the Easter season.
4. Observe the days of fasting and abstinence established by the Church.
5. Help to provide for the needs of the Church.

Regarding the first precept, it must be said that purposely missing Mass on Sunday or a holy day of obligation is a mortal sin. We say "purposely" because while it is a grave matter to miss Mass when required to go, for the sin to be committed, one must know it is Sunday or a holy day of obligation and, knowing this, choose not to go even though there are no extenuating circumstances (such as illness that prevents one from attending).

This is true, in fact, for all sin: one must both know it is wrong and freely choose it in order for what is in itself sinful to be an actual sin. But there are sins, and then there are sins. The classic division among them, and the really important distinction, is between mortal sins and venial sins.

The three conditions necessary for committing a mortal sin are (1) that it be grave matter, (2) that the person has full knowledge, and (3) that he or she gives deliberate consent.

If the matter of the sin is not grave or serious but of smaller import, then the sin is called venial, which comes from the Latin term (*venia*) for "forgiveness," meaning that this sin is excusable, pardonable, forgivable. Not that mortal sins are not forgivable, but their forgiveness requires more effort on our part—namely, going to Confession and receiving absolution from the priest in the name of Christ and the Church.

What are examples of venial sins? We already mentioned the classic example of stealing gum from the store. St. Anthony Mary Claret mentions the sin of introducing talk about another's defects. In my own life I constantly struggle with the sarcastic comment that isn't merely funny but is actually hurtful because it's an expression of anger, impatience, or annoyance. St. Thomas Aquinas is clear in his teaching that any sort of lie (words that deliberately contradict the truth) is a sin, and if the matter is not serious, this would be a venial sin.

The important thing to remember is that we are all prone to sins of every kind: big, little, horrible, and almost funny. What we want to do is become ever more aware of how good God is, how much He loves us, and how much happier both we and He will be if we reject temptation and sin. When we find, though, that we have foolishly given in to sin, it is a great privilege to be able to go to Confession. Here, with the priest in the place of Jesus, we can admit our commissions and omissions (what we have done wrong and what we have failed to do right) and receive His abundant forgiveness.

You can see why the second precept of the Church is to confess our sins once a year. Technically this is not required if one is not in the state of mortal sin, but it is the consensus of the wise that going to Confession will keep us from falling into mortal sin as well as wash our souls clean. In particular, it is a laudable practice to go to Confession during Advent, in preparation for receiving Jesus at Christmas, and in Lent, in preparation for Easter and our Easter Communion.

It may seem strange that the next precept is to receive Holy Communion at least once a year in the Easter season. We live in an age when refraining from Communion is less a concern than it used to be, although unfortunately it is an age when refraining from Confession is all too common. The Church, being our Mother and our teacher, knows to link these two sacraments of Confession and the Holy Eucharist together, that we may receive Him in the best possible disposition, into the cleanest possible soul.

The fourth precept of the Church is to observe the days of fasting and abstinence established by the Church. To fast means, in this context, to eat only one main meal; in her mercy, the Church allows for two smaller meals on fasting days as well as the main meal, but together the two smaller meals should not exceed the main meal, and no eating in between. Abstinence, here, means not eating meat.

Why would the Church want us to fast and abstain? These are ancient practices that help us enter into the mystery of Christ, and in particular they are signs of penance that go with penitential times. The Church's penitential days and times are all Fridays throughout the year and the forty days of Lent.

The current days of fasting for all Roman Catholics aged eighteen to fifty-nine (this excludes those younger and older, as well as pregnant and nursing mothers and the sick) are only two: Ash Wednesday (the first day of Lent) and Good Friday (the day on which Christ was crucified and died for us, the Friday before Easter Sunday). On these days, abstinence from meat is also required for those fourteen and older.

As far as other days of abstinence, there is a current confusion, but it's one that is easily cleared up.

Just like all Sundays of the year are little Easters, marking the day of Our Lord's Resurrection, so all Fridays of the year are penitential days in honor of Jesus' dying on Good Friday. The exception to this is when a solemnity—like Christmas— falls on a Friday, thus changing it from a fast to a feast.

It used to be part of Church law that Roman Catholics abstained from meat on all Fridays of the year. (The Eastern Catholic rites have their own customs and laws, as we will mention in a later chapter.) The new regulations for Roman Catholics are spelled out in the 1983 *Code of Canon Law* and still require abstinence on every Friday of the year for those fourteen years and older, but this law is followed by another that allows bishops' conferences to specify more particularly the observance of fast, abstinence, "and other forms of penance, especially works of charity and exercises of piety."

Thus the U.S. bishops' conference, with the approval of Rome, has prescribed that on Fridays outside of Lent, Catholics in the United States *may substitute* another act of penance or a charitable practice of their own choosing for the more standard practice of abstinence from meat.

In other words, Fridays throughout the year are still penitential days, but instead of giving up meat on Fridays, you can give up something else or do a good work or say some extra prayers.

Traditionally, Catholics offered their Friday abstinence from meat for the souls in purgatory. This is still a salutary custom, only now each Friday we have the option to help the poor souls to heaven by offering another sacrifice or good work joined to the supreme sacrifice of Christ on the Cross. Our sacrifice or good work is especially beneficial because we do it through obedience to this precept and the law of the Church.

Because we are creatures of habit, many Catholics find it easiest simply to abstain from meat every Friday of the year. That way, the penance is done; built into the typical Friday, it is not forgotten, nor does one need to come up with a new penance or good work or prayer each succeeding week.

The fifth precept, to help provide for the needs of the Church, does not specify how much one must contribute, but a standard and ancient practice is to tithe 10 percent of one's income. This 10 percent tithe goes all the way back to Abram's offering to the priest Melchizedek (Genesis 14:20) and has the advantage of scriptural endorsement.

However large or small that 10 percent is, one can give it in a number of ways—to the local parish in the Sunday collection, to the poor through St. Vincent de Paul Society, to authentically Catholic schools, to the missions, and the list goes on.

If you are able to give more than 10 percent, you will be giving freely from what God has so generously given to you, just as Christ recommends in the Gospel. If you are living below the poverty line, 10 percent will be a big chunk of what is needed just for basic necessities. But if you are the Queen of Sheba, you have plenty of loot to spare, and because the Church does not specify any particular amount we need to give, you are free to give plenty. In the words of Our Lord,

> Fear not, little flock, for it is your Father's good pleasure to give you the kingdom. Sell your possessions, and give to the needy. Provide yourselves with moneybags that do not grow old, with a treasure in the heavens that does not fail, where no thief approaches and no moth destroys. For where your treasure is, there will be your heart also. (Luke 12:32–34)

I have a friend who heeded Christ's advice and gave the majority of his inheritance to the poor. Far from regretting it, he liked to repeat in later years, "It was the best investment I ever made!"

Chapter 6

How to Go to Confession

Confession is a sacrament of mercy. That is why people should approach the confessional with confidence and joy.

— St. Jacinta Marto

If our sins are venial, we go to Confession to wipe away the slight stains they leave on our souls, as well as to lessen the punishment they deserve, and then, too, to gain grace, which gives us strength to resist sin in the future.

If our sins are mortal, we rush to Confession to formally invite God back into our souls. Don't be afraid: God loves you infinitely and longs for you beyond measure. Plus, on the human side, priests are here to give us the sacraments, so if the churches around you do not offer frequent opportunities for Confession, call and make an appointment. Embarrassing? Perhaps, but it's a small price to pay to get right with God, and you don't have to tell the parish receptionist your sins, just that you need to see Father for Confession ASAP! Meanwhile, do your best to make a perfect act of contrition, or make whatever kind you can, and trust Him to meet you in this sacrament with the fullness of His mercy.

I have heard it said, "Pray as if everything depended on God; work as if everything depended on you." I don't like this saying because I prefer to pray as if everything depended on God, and work as if everything depended on Him too, but the least I can do is my small part. But in a parallel format to this saying, let me advise you to confess as if you are confessing to Christ, the Spouse of your soul, but receive the words of the priest (besides the absolution, which he gives in the name of Christ) as if they are the words of a man. That is, if you find that the priest is misreading your soul—since not everyone has the gifts of St. John Vianney and St. Padre Pio—or is impatient with you, leave that behind in the confessional, and take with you the awesome forgiveness that the power of his priesthood and his union with Christ make possible.

So how do you make this work well?

Here are the conditions of a good Confession:

1. Knowledge of your sins. This requires an examination of conscience. Ask your guardian angel and the Holy Spirit for enlightenment, and consider the time since your last Confession and what sins you have committed.

2. Sorrow for your sins, with a firm purpose of amendment—that is, the determination not to commit them again.

3. Confession of your sins to the priest. For mortal sins, make a clear Confession of each sin and the number of times committed; for venial sins, list them perhaps by type and number (such as "I sinned against charity on three different occasions when I gossiped with my neighbor"), but venial sins do not need to all be named to be forgiven, as mortal sins do.

4. Doing the penance the priest gives you. Usually the penance consists of prayers, such as saying an Our Father and a Hail Mary, but sometimes the priest can get creative, and you may also be required to make satisfaction for your sins, such as paying for the gum you stole or returning the $10,000 to the bank.

A note on the examination of conscience: the two extremes to be avoided are laxity and scrupulosity. Laxity would include refusing to acknowledge certain sins as sins and also excusing yourself from all sorts of sins by explaining them away (to yourself or to the priest) by a multitude of circumstances. Scrupulosity, by contrast, is the mistake of accusing oneself of wrongdoing in matters that are not sinful. This can become a spiritual disease or habitual problem that plagues the penitent, making sin appear everywhere and causing the suffering person to refrain from Communion under the misapprehension that he or she is in a state of mortal sin.

One might think that laxity is a much bigger problem than scrupulosity, since our society does not recognize or acknowledge most sin and in fact even allows, prescribes, or rewards many grievous sins. My own experience of the past forty years is that once a person has a conversion or reversion to the Catholic Faith (this latter term, "reversion" refers to the return to the fervent practice of the Faith), laxity quickly flees and before long scrupulosity may take its place. The helpful principle laid down by the Church's great moral Doctor, St. Alphonsus de Liguori, is that when one is in doubt about an action being a sin, performing that action cannot be a sin.

Do not confuse this principle with wishing something was not a sin or trying to will away its sinfulness. It does not apply, for instance, to robbing a bank and hoping that taking merely $1,000 is not serious. Instead, it is a principle intended to help the scrupulous soul who worries, after receiving Communion, that perhaps her watch is showing a different time from the family's kitchen clock and her fast before Communion was really only fifty-five minutes and not the prescribed hour.

Let's say you have examined your conscience, perhaps using the Ten Commandments and the precepts of the Church as your guide, or maybe with the help of a handy list found at the back of the church, in a prayer book, or on a Catholic

website. You wait your turn for the confessional. In a traditional box confessional there is a light above each door. When
the light is on where the priest sits, that means he is there.
When you see another light on, that means someone is kneeling, either already confessing or waiting to confess. You know
it is your turn when there is an unlit light, or when you see
an open door to one of the boxes (or to the reconciliation
room), or when the person ahead of you exits the confessional
(or room).

In you go! Kneel down (or sit, if you are going to confess
face-to-face and there is an empty chair for you facing the
priest in his chair), and bless yourself. The priest may say some
welcoming words, but if not (or after he does), it is your turn
to speak. Don't worry; this is not hard. I still use the formula
I learned as a little girl, and though it's not the only way to
go to Confession, it is a standard and effective (and stress-
reducing) way that I am happy to share with you here:

> Bless me, Father, for I have sinned. I am a _____ [fill in the
> blank with your state in life: for instance, I say I am a wife
> and mother. You might say, "I am a student" or "I am a single
> young person" or "I am twelve," as the case may be]. It has been
> _____ [fill in the amount of time: for instance, "one month"]
> since my last confession, and these are my sins....

You then state your sins, by kind and number. If you have
any mortal sins, state them first, by kind and number, getting
them out in the open, where they will do no more harm. Then
name whatever venial sins you have to confess.

After you have stated your sins, conclude by saying, "I am
sorry for these and all my sins."

With any luck, the priest will now say something kind and
reassuring, such as, "That is a good and humble confession."
Or he may want clarification on something you said and ask

a question. For instance, before I got in the habit of stating that I was a wife and mother, one time I was confessing "wife and mother" type sins when—because I have a very young-sounding voice—the priest jumped in after I said, "I am sorry for these and all my sins," with "*How old are you?*" This naturally led to a very awkward conversation because I immediately rounded up to the nearest important sounding age—I think I was forty-three and said, "Forty-five"—but then I realized I was lying to the priest in the confessional! So I backed down to forty-four but remembered I was actually forty-three, if I am remembering rightly.

I have a feeling other people don't get themselves in these kinds of jams, but the long and short of it is, do tell the priest a little about yourself at the outset. That way, when you sound like you are fourteen and say you were short-tempered with your husband, he will know that the sin is one against charity, not disobedience to your parents—who, no doubt, don't realize their fourteen-year-old is married.

In any case, answer as simply and clearly as you can—and do remember to speak loudly enough for the priest to hear you but not so loudly that everyone outside the confessional hears you too. Then the priest may give you advice, and since he has the grace of the priesthood and perhaps much experience behind him (both his own and others', since if he is an older priest, he may have heard thousands of Confessions in his time), it behooves you to listen carefully. You will often hear exactly what you need to hear. If not, no matter; you are immersing yourself in God's mercy.

Keep your ears open to hear the penance the priest gives you, and then he will usually ask you to make an Act of Contrition. This is a great prayer; it might be printed right there in the confessional, but if you don't know an Act of Contrition by heart, copy out the one in the last chapter of this book and bring it with you so you are ready. This is your chance to express your sorrow for your sins and really firm up that purpose of amendment. I like to focus with all my might (and since I have about a four-second attention span, this means a lot to me and God) on the last part of the first sentence, italicized here: "O my God, I am heartily sorry for having offended Thee, and I detest all my sins because of Thy just punishments, *but most of all because they offend Thee, my God, who art all good and deserving of all my love . . .*"

The priest will give you absolution, and you will hear some of the most beautiful words in the human language: "God, the Father of mercies, through the death and resurrection of His Son has reconciled the world to Himself and sent the Holy Spirit among us for the forgiveness of sins; through the ministry of the Church may God give you pardon and peace, and I absolve you from your sins in the name of the Father, and of the Son, and of the Holy Spirit."

It is possible the priest may say the first part of this formula while you are saying your Act of Contrition, but he will save those very essential words at the end for after you have completed your prayer, in which case you will hear, simply, "I absolve you from your sins in the name of the Father, and of the Son, and of the Holy Spirit."

To this you may add a rousing (but not too rousing, lest you frighten those waiting outside) "Amen."

The priest will then dismiss you with words such as these: "The Lord has freed you from your sins. Go in peace," to which you might reply, simply, "Thank you, Father," and exit.

If he begins his dismissal with, "Give thanks to the Lord, for He is good," you respond, "And His mercy endures forever."

You have one last thing to do—or more completely, two.

Find a spot to pray. Usually you will make your confession in church, and now that you've left the confessional or reconciliation room, go near the tabernacle or perhaps near a particularly endearing statue of a saint you love. Kneel, and say your penance. That's the first and most important thing you need to do.

But secondly, this is a really great moment for you and God. He has cleansed you with His sanctifying precious blood. He has freed you from your sins and made you—once again—a beautiful new creation. Thank Him! Open your soul to Him with an outpouring of gratitude, love, or just plain chitchat. If you loved what the priest said to you, tell Jesus so and thank Him! If you are not thrilled with what the priest had to offer (other than absolution), tell Jesus that. But most of all, take a second to realize the newfound union with your Beloved, or the closer union His mercy has brought about. You are His, entirely. Enjoy it and let Him enjoy you. Take a deep breath, flash Jesus a smile, and feel the lightness of your new, clean self.

Chapter 7

Marriage, Weddings, and
Happily Ever After

*Great are the joys in marriage, as there is the lifting of progressive
veils, until one is brought into the blazing lights of the Presence
of God.*

—Archbishop Fulton Sheen

The modern world has made mincemeat of marriage. But the
Catholic Church has saved every last speck of its beauty and
wonder, so if you are not Catholic, her teachings and laws on
marriage are enough to draw you into the shelter of her maternal arms, and if you are Catholic, thank your lucky stars and
God Himself, who is the giver of every good gift.

St. Paul, in his Letter to the Ephesians, after explaining
how spouses are to behave toward each other, quotes Genesis:
"Therefore a man shall leave his father and mother and hold
fast to his wife, and the two shall become one flesh." He then
continues, "This mystery is profound, and I am saying that
it refers to Christ and the church," (5:31–32), or as the New
American Bible has it, "This is a great mystery, but I speak in
reference to Christ and the church."

Truly this Sacrament of Marriage is a great sacrament and
a great mystery, symbolizing and representing as it does the
union of the Bridegroom Christ and His Bride, the Church.

I am alternately amused and horrified by the way our age has descended from somewhat understandable mistakes about marriage, remarriage, the role of marital relations (within marriage and without), and the like to the complete denial of nature and gender.

And yet hear what the *Catechism* says, quoting from the ancient author and Father of the Church Tertullian (who wrote this in about the year 200):

> How can I ever express the happiness of a marriage joined by the Church, strengthened by an offering, sealed by a blessing, announced by angels, and ratified by the Father? . . . How wonderful the bond between two believers, now one in hope, one in desire, one in discipline, one in the same service! They are both children of one Father and servants of the same Master, undivided in spirit and flesh, truly two in one flesh. Where the flesh is one, one also is the spirit. (*CCC*, 1642)

So what is the truth? What is the real deal about marriage? Happily, the Church does not leave us to our own devices or ability to sort out the confusion we find ourselves in, no matter what era. People may quibble about whether this is the perfect enunciation, but here is a fairly complete definition of marriage from the *Code of Canon Law*:

> The matrimonial covenant, by which a man and a woman establish between themselves a partnership of the whole of life, is by its nature ordered toward the good of the spouses and the procreation and education of offspring; this covenant between baptized persons has been raised by Christ the Lord to the dignity of a sacrament. (canon 1055)

In plain English, marriage is a sacramental bond between a baptized man and a baptized woman; this bond lasts until one of the spouses dies; and it is for the sake of getting each other to heaven (which is the spouses' truest good) and for having children and raising them for heaven too.

Further exploration of Church tradition, teaching, and law reveals that marriage is exclusive—only one wife per husband, and vice versa—and faithful, which means we have not forgotten the sixth and ninth commandments: no marital relations with someone who is not your spouse.

In regard to openness to life and the bearing of children, it is the perennial (that means lasting and forever) teaching of the Church, in accord with natural law, that artificial contraception is never an option.

Following the natural cycles of a woman's fertility so as to prudently cooperate with God in conceiving or postponing the conception of children, however, is allowed, since it is in accord with nature and respectful of the union of the marital act and of its primary end.

Will following these rules make you happy? Yes.

Will disobeying them lead you into trouble in this life and the next? Yes, too.

Is it really that simple? Yes, yes, yes.

Is it easy?

Well, that depends. For some it is; for some it isn't. But it is true, and it will lead to happiness much more quickly than launching your own worldview or following the latest fashion.

So let's say you have met "the one" and are planning to get married. What do you need to know?

As with everything treated in this book, you will find much more information in the *Catechism of the Catholic Church*, the *Code of Canon Law*, and the Bible. But with respect to marriage in particular, the Church offers three additional exquisite documents: *Casti Connubii* (On Christian Marriage) by Pope Pius XI, *Humanae Vitae* (Of Human Life) by Pope St. Paul VI, and *Familiaris Consortio* (On the Role of the Christian

Family in the Modern World) by Pope St. John Paul II. These
are well worth reading, and *Humane Vitae* in particular is
essential reading.

For now, in the limited space of this book, here are a few
thoughts on weddings—especially meant for those getting
married—that you might not find in other places.

First, as I mentioned above and as I learned many years ago
before my own wedding: the Bride is the Church. Yes, this is
figurative, and yet so important.

When you are at a wedding in a Catholic church, and the
bridesmaids have come down the aisle, and the back door
has closed, but then it opens again and the whole congregation stands and turns to see the bride enter, it is to see the
most beautiful sight on this earth: the Church, dressed for her
Bridegroom and Spouse, Jesus Christ. That is why the bride
wears spotless white (or a lovely ivory)—in this moment as
she represents the Church, she is spotless!

Might I suggest, then, that the wedding dress be modest
as well as beautiful? If it does not cover the shoulders and the
back, there are all sorts of wraps a bride might wear, along
with a long veil, to more perfectly symbolize the Church in
her chaste and perfectly modest beauty.

My second suggestion is—if you are the bride, the groom,
or a parent of the bride or groom—to focus on the wedding
itself, rather than the reception, when planning. Yes, I know
the reception will need lots of planning! But so does the wedding, and it is fitting for us to spend as much time in our
preparation to receive the sacrament as we spend on preparing
to receive our guests. While a welcoming reception is an integral part of the wedding celebration, it is second in importance to the sacrament itself.

Bride and groom: take care in your choice of the priest who
will marry you, and the music and flowers that will help lift
hearts to God. You will have a choice of readings, as well as

hymns. Spend time together making those readings a reflection of what is in your hearts, or what you hope will be.

For those attending a wedding, a similar suggestion: while it is wonderful to take care to look nice for the wedding, to bring or send a suitable gift, and so on, most important of all to the bride and groom (whether they know it or not) are your prayers. Say a Rosary for them in the week before the wedding or at the wedding or during their honeymoon. Or perhaps go to your parish church and arrange with the receptionist for a Mass to be said for the newly married couple. They need your prayers even more than your gift—far more than whatever they have on their registry! And speaking of their gift registry, while it is considerate to buy them something they have chosen, another option is to buy the newly married a crucifix, a family Bible, or a spiritual book you think will help them on their way.

To the couple who will be married—here are two final things you should know:

First, marriage is "until death do you part." This is why you have had a courtship and engagement and some marriage preparation program (this last is required by the Church). Talk to each other and be sure you both understand that these vows are, in effect, forever for at least one of you—the one who dies first!

Although baptized as a baby, I remember clearly when, at the age of eighteen, I went from living in the world to being fully Catholic—knowing, understanding, and accepting Church teaching. One of the most striking things about my newfound knowledge had to do with marriage. I realized that if both spouses in a marriage knew and believed that marriage is permanent and lasts until the death of one of the spouses, that marriage would be an entirely different thing (a sacrament, I now see) than if even one of them was entering into Holy Matrimony with the idea that "hopefully it will work out."

Be sure you and your prospective spouse understand and accept this truth!

Second, using artificial birth control is not an option. Be sure you both understand and agree on this, too, before you get married. Many recommend that you learn natural family planning before you get married so that if you need to use it in marriage, you will already be familiar with it. I would say at least look into it and find out where you can get the information and education in it if you need it. But first and foremost, know and commit to the Church's teaching on this important—indeed, crucial—aspect of marriage.

A personal note: My husband and I scared a lot of my extended family when our reply to their "How many kids do you want?" was "As many as God sends!" They were all convinced we would have a dozen children at least. But in the event, God wanted for us only two.

You never know what God's plan is. We also live in a wonderful time when, if He is sending children more quickly than a married couple can handle, there are extremely scientific, accurate, reliable, and natural ways to postpone pregnancy. Similarly, if He is sending children more slowly than a married couple's desire for them, they can use this same knowledge to possibly help Him send them faster.

Have you ever laughed at one of those awful commercials for various drugs, wherein the advertisers have combined scenic views and smiling, happy, gamboling patients with a quiet, soothing voice-over telling you that the side effects of these same drugs may include nausea, vomiting, hair loss, insanity, and death? You don't need to waste your time exploring the hideous side effects of artificial contraception. I can tell you briefly that many of them "may include" some truly horrible things, including, for some versions of the birth control pill, abortion. At the very least they definitely include a parting of ways with nature and the Church, your truest guide to reality, and they may include a parting of the ways with your spouse because when you choose artificial birth control, you have rejected one of the essential aspects of marriage and an essential part of your spouse.

So, convince each other of the truth of the Church's teaching (if either of you need convincing), and remember, too, that this means no sterilization of either of you, and if you are unable to conceive, no artificial/intrusive (taking the marriage act out of the marriage bed) interventions. Did I really have to add that? I did, and it is no reflection on you that our times require much basic education that sometimes doesn't come until one is long past school days.

The principle is, simply, that in marrying, you accept the other person "for better, for worse, for richer, for poorer, in sickness and in health, to love and to cherish, till death do us part." Both "health" and "cherish" imply that you accept the other person's amazing gift of fertility, and that's that.

I also must add here that another amazing gift, the gift of faith that we receive at Baptism, and which is strengthened at Confirmation, actually includes within it by definition the acceptance of and adherence to all the Church's teaching. As the *Catechism* puts it,

> Faith is first of all a personal adherence of man to God. At the same time, and inseparably, it is a *free assent to the whole truth that God has revealed....* It is right and just to entrust oneself wholly to God and to believe absolutely what he says. It would be futile and false to place such faith in a creature. (*CCC*, 150)

In other words, you do already believe these things in virtue of being Catholic. It's best, however, in these confusing times, to be sure you and your spouse both know what you believe. Know, that is, what the Church teaches so that you may more easily live it out together and thus be assured of the "happily ever after" that follows the wedding day.

Chapter 8

The Rest of the Story on Marriage

Young husbands should say to their wives: "I have taken you in my arms, I love you, I prefer you to my life itself. For the present life is nothing and my most ardent dream is to spend it with you in such a way that we may be assured of not being separated in the life reserved for us."

—St. John Chrysostom

We have talked about marriages that end with happily ever after. But what about marriages that fail?

Not to be a downer, but there is more you need to know, not only to navigate your own marriage if that is your state in life, but also to provide whatever first aid you can to those you love who find themselves in difficult situations.

So what can we say about failed marriages?

Strictly speaking, marriages that seemingly fail fall into two categories: (1) those that were never marriages to begin with and (2) those in which the spouses face hardships that require, for their own well-being and that of the children, separation.

The first case need not surprise us. Since there are essential requirements for marriage, when these requirements have not been fulfilled, there is no marriage. Then, if asked, the Church can investigate and judge that there never was a marriage. This is what happens when a couple gets an annulment, which is most decidedly not "Catholic divorce" but rather a determination that this union never was a marriage.

The *Code of Canon Law*, which governs Roman Catholics, has seven sections. The fourth of these is on the sacraments, and each has its own section of laws. The shortest of these sections is on the Anointing of the Sick and contains only ten canons, or laws. The second longest section is on the Blessed Eucharist and contains sixty-one canons. Can you guess which sacrament gets the most laws?

Hands down, the Sacrament of Marriage has the most with an astounding 102 canons. This means that Holy Mother Church is very careful in her explanations, requirements, directives, and the recourses provided regarding this "great sacrament," as St. Paul called it. And this is why, even when the Church's annulment process is simplified, there is nothing too simple about it. This is also the case for her counsels and preparation for marriage. None of this is taken lightly by the Church because the majority of her children will be married, and she wants them to do it well and properly with all the graces the sacrament provides.

Because marriage requires lifelong fidelity, two reasons for a non-marriage (impediments that cause the nullity of what is intended to be a marriage) are (1) if one of the spouses enters the marriage with no intention of a lifelong commitment and (2) if one enters with no intention of fidelity to the other. Similarly, because marriage is for the sake of the procreation and education of children, if one of the spouses enters marriage with an intention to never have children, there is, then, no sacramental marriage.

These are not, however, things you can determine on your own. When you have cause to believe a marriage is null, that it never was and could never be a marriage due to some impediment, then you approach the Church and follow the established procedures so that she can determine and inform you of the existential situation (if you are truly married or not).

The reason this is not "Catholic divorce" is that divorce means you were once legally married and now you are not. Divorce is a declaration of civil law. But an annulment is a declaration of Church law that you were not sacramentally married to begin with.

There is such a thing, too, as a civil annulment, but this means you were not married in the eyes of the law (though it seemed you were). This is different from Catholic annulment, which declares that whether or not you were properly civilly married, you are not and have not been, in this apparent marriage, actually and sacramentally married.

If a couple has grounds for annulment (that is, they think there are impediments that prevented their marriage), they must first get a civil divorce before they apply for an annulment.

If a couple seeks an annulment and the Church judges that there is no cause and, in fact, they are married, they may continue to live separately (and with a civil divorce), but they may not remarry because they are still married to each other and will be until one of the spouses dies.

There are also situations in which the couple realizes they have a valid sacramental marriage (are truly married), but they cannot live together. Due to Original Sin and personal sin, this world and all of us in it are rather wounded, imperfect, and sometimes incapable of living closely together. A marriage might fail in this sense if one of the spouses is abusive to the other or to the children, or if one of the spouses has become mentally ill. This does not mean that suddenly the marriage is invalid, but it may mean that the spouses cannot live together.

Chapter IX of the canons on marriage is "The Separation of the Spouses" and begins with canon 1141: "A marriage which is ratified and consummated cannot be dissolved by any human power or by any cause other than death." The *Code* then gives laws for "dissolution of the bond" and, in the following subsection, for "separation while the bond remains."

What every Catholic should know about marriage, then, is that it is a great sacrament and mystery, not to be entered upon lightly, because it cannot be exited lightly! In situations where "happily ever after" does not come true, the truth of the marriage itself may still be quite real. Then although separation may be necessary (and consult canon law to understand more about that), the separated spouses are in reality married, though unable to live together. The marriage is itself a sign of Christ's fidelity to His Church, and as such requires our own fidelity to it. Even when spouses live separately, they are not free to contract other marriages or live as if they are.

Does this mean marriage is a terribly frightening prospect? Not at all. Quite the contrary, it is the dream of most people for a very good reason: because with God's grace, it is full of beauty, love, joy, and often romance.

Our older son spent three months in Russia a few years ago and found himself one Saturday morning in a café, in the university town of Kazan, with an English-speaking club consisting of Russian young people. The topic they had chosen for discussion that morning was marriage.

Our son, twenty-two and unmarried, enjoyed the conversation immensely, participating judiciously, occasionally tossing in comments on what marriage was and what it required. By the end of the discussion, the sum of his remarks added up to the full truth about marriage.

One of the young Russians said, "Such a beautiful idea! To live with one person, faithful to each other, having children together, raising them together, one in this union until you die—we all want that!" The others nodded. "But it is not real! Where could anyone find that?"

"That's easy," our son said. "My parents and all their friends live this way. I've grown up with this kind of marriage around me. I know it is possible because everyone we know has this."

The group was stunned but could hardly argue.

My husband and I are, necessarily, much older than our son, and we have seen many more marriages than he has. With sorrow I report that even among the most faithful Catholics, we have seen marriages that have grounds for annulment, we have seen the subsequent judgment of the Church declaring these marriages null, and we have seen other marriages that have failed in the sense of requiring separation even though the marriage is valid—and the spouses, heroically, continue to live in fidelity to their marriage vows.

Compared to the statistics for marriage in the world, these numbers in the Church are very low. We have seen many more marriages that are brilliant as diamonds, full of peace and joy, living witnesses to the love of Christ and His Church for one another. Our Lord and His Church do not fail us, and the grace of this sacrament is tremendous.

One important thing to remember is that the grace of marriage is ongoing. If you are married and in a time of stress and strain, ask for more grace. Ask Our Lady and St. Joseph to intercede for you, and ask our Savior to pour out His love upon you.

Recently the Church canonized a married couple. This was not the first time in her history that she had recognized the sanctity of both spouses in a marriage, but it was the first time a couple was canonized in one process, precisely as the two-become-one. Their canonization took place on World Mission Sunday, a fitting day because this couple, Louis and Zélie Martin, were the parents of the patroness of the missions, St. Thérèse of Lisieux.

Their daughter's sanctity didn't appear out of nowhere. It was the fruit of their love and faithfulness to Christ and the

Church. They had another daughter, Leonie, who may some-day be declared a saint also. She was the problem child and "ugly duckling" of their brood, but thanks to their love (and her sister's), she became happy and holy even in this life.

We are surrounded by clouds of witnesses to the sanctity of marriage and the joys of family life. May God continue to raise up droves of saints from the ranks of the married. Who knows? Perhaps you and your spouse will be among them.

Chapter 9

What to Make of Mary

I wish to go to Jerusalem, if you will permit me, to see the holy faithful who are there, especially Mary, the Mother of Jesus, who is said to be admired and loved by all. For what friend of our faith ... would not be delighted to see and speak to her who brought forth the true God?

—St. Ignatius of Antioch
(writing to St. John the Evangelist)

St. Luke, not one of the original twelve Apostles, but a medical doctor, disciple of St. Paul, and author of the third Gospel and Acts of the Apostles, knew Mary personally.

He tells us at the beginning of his Gospel that the things he knows were from "eyewitnesses and ministers of the word [who] have delivered them to us," and then he recounts details about the visit by an angel to Zechariah and later to Mary, followed by Mary's visit to St. Elizabeth and the conversation these two holy pregnant women had. Next he tells of the birth of St. John the Baptist and what was said on that occasion, most notably by John's father, Zechariah, when his tongue was loosed and he could speak after nine months of enforced silence. Finally, in these first chapters of his Gospel, St. Luke describes the birth of Jesus in a stable in Bethlehem, His naming, His presentation in the Temple according to the Jewish law, and what happened when His family returned to the Temple in His twelfth year.

Twice in this account, the events of which are found almost exclusively in his Gospel, St. Luke tells us, "But Mary treasured up all these things, pondering them in her heart," and again, "His mother treasured up all these things in her heart" (Luke 2:19, 51). We can logically conclude that Mary was one of those early eyewitnesses from whom Luke received his information. And to help our argument, there is the long-standing tradition of the Church (which goes back to Gospel days) that Mary was the source of Luke's knowledge of these events.

Let's consider for a moment the visit of Mary to her cousin St. Elizabeth, which we read in Luke's Gospel. Mary is carrying in her womb baby Jesus, and Elizabeth is pregnant with his cousin John. But no one on earth knows of Mary's pregnancy. There were no cell phones or even telegrams in those days, no Pony Express. Mary makes a surprise visit to her older pregnant cousin, who would always give her a warm welcome, but especially now in Elizabeth's time of confinement.

What happens when Mary arrives? She enters the house and greets Elizabeth.

> And when Elizabeth heard the greeting of Mary, the baby leaped in her womb. And Elizabeth was filled with the Holy Spirit, and she exclaimed with a loud cry, "Blessed are you among women and blessed is the fruit of your womb! And why is this granted to me that the mother of my Lord should come to me? For behold, when the sound of your greeting came to my ears, the baby in my womb leaped for joy. And blessed is she who believed that there would be a fulfillment of what was spoken to her from the Lord." (Luke 1:41–45)

Those words from Elizabeth might sound familiar—"Blessed are you among women and blessed is the fruit of your womb"—because they are part of the Hail Mary. But why is

Elizabeth so excited? What is it that alerts her to the wonderful news Mary has not yet shared with her?

We could think it was the leap of St. John in her womb, and I'm sure that was part of it. But listen to her words: "Why is this granted me, that the mother of my Lord should come to me?"

St. Luke did not really need to tell us Elizabeth was filled with the Holy Spirit. How else could she have known, first, that Mary is expecting and, second, that Mary is expecting God?

What Elizabeth is so excited about is that Mary is the Mother of God. If this sounds crazy to you, know that it is not just you. Heads have been split over this one, councils have met, and it became a raging controversy in the early centuries of the Church, whether you could even say it—namely, that Mary is the Mother of God.

Mary is the Mother of Jesus. Jesus is God. Therefore, Mary is the Mother of God.

So far so good, but the problems came when some wanted to make clear that Mary was not the originator of God. Again, so far so good, but deeper down, it turned out that some wanted to deny the union of Christ's two natures, and they wanted to identify Mary as the Mother of Christ but not as the Mother of God.

St. Cyril of Alexandria explained that a mother gives birth to a person, not a nature, and so with his help, in the year 431 at the Council of Ephesus, the Church officially settled the question: Jesus is one Divine person with two natures, His mother's human nature and His Father's divine nature. He has always been and will always be the second Person of the Most Holy Trinity, but since, as St. Cyril pointed out, a mother gives birth to a person, not a nature, Mary, in giving birth to Jesus, God and man, is indeed the Mother of God (*Theotokos*, in Greek).

It is Mary's motherhood, and in particular her motherhood of Our Lord, that is at the root of Catholic devotion to her. But there is another side of her motherhood that equally awakens our love.

Do you remember those words of Jesus from the Cross? St. John, the Beloved Disciple (brother of Andrew, rather than the Baptist), is our eyewitness this time. He writes in the nineteenth chapter of his Gospel, "When Jesus saw his mother and the disciple whom he loved standing nearby, he said to his mother, 'Woman, behold, your son!' And he said to the disciple, 'Behold, your mother!' " (John 19:26–27).

When God says something, it is. On the very first page of the Bible we read, "And God said, 'Let there be light'; and there was light" (Genesis 1:3). When Jesus says to the dead Lazarus, "Come out," Lazarus comes out (John 11:43–44). As St. Thomas Aquinas tells us in his eucharistic hymn *Adoro Te Devote*, "Truth Himself speaks truly, or there's nothing true." And so when Our Lord says in His dying words, "Behold your mother," and "Behold your son," He again effects what He speaks: Mary becomes Mother of all mankind, and every person becomes her child.

Mary is such a big deal to us, then, because she is our Mother. If you have had the loving care of your natural mother or an adoptive mother, you understand to some degree what a mother does. If your mother was not able or willing to provide you with loving care, you may be even more aware of the importance of a mom. And no matter how loving any of our mothers are, they fall far short of Mary. She is the Mother of mothers, the most maternal creature God ever made, sinless, immaculate: perfect in her purity, her unselfishness, her intimacy with God, and her power over His Heart.

Think about it: a good man will do whatever he can to fulfill his good mother's requests, and this man, Jesus, can do everything. There are very few words of Mary reported in the four Gospels, but among them are her words to Jesus at the wedding feast of Cana—"They have no wine"—and her subsequent words to the stewards when, though He initially seemed to resist her request, she had full confidence in Her Son's merciful love. And so she instructed them, "Do whatever he tells you" (John 2:1–5).

Because she is Mother of the King of kings, Mary is also the Queen Mother. St. John saw her as such in the vision he recounts in Revelation: "And a great sign appeared in heaven, a woman clothed with the sun, with the moon under her feet, and on her head a crown of twelve stars" (Revelation 12:1).

There is a mystery of the Holy Rosary and a feast in the liturgical calendar to celebrate the coronation of Mary as Queen of Heaven and Earth. In her litany, too, we invoke Mary under many different titles, many of them referring to her as Queen. These titles in Mary's honor have been added over time as her children glory in articulating their Mother's honor and honoring her privileges. But to present more formally the chief prerogatives of Mary, here are the four Marian dogmas.

Her Immaculate Conception

Unlike all other descendants of Adam and Eve, Mary's soul did not have the stain of Original Sin that the rest of us have inherited from our first parents. Mary's Immaculate Conception was formally defined on December 8, 1854, by Blessed Pope Pius IX, who declared "the Blessed Virgin Mary to have been, from the first instant of her conception, by a singular grace and privilege of Almighty God, in view of the merits of Christ Jesus the Savior of Mankind, preserved free from all stain of original sin" (*Ineffabilis Deus*).

Mary's Immaculate Conception is not to be confused with the conception of Jesus in her womb.

The Virgin Birth and Mary's Perpetual Virginity

As we say in the Creed, Jesus "was conceived by the power of the Holy Spirit and born of the Virgin Mary."

This is the Virgin Birth (Mary's giving birth to Jesus), not to be confused with the Immaculate Conception, which refers to Mary's conception without Original Sin in the womb of her mother, St. Anne.

In conjunction with the Virgin Birth, Mary's perpetual virginity means three things. As St. Augustine explains in one of his sermons, which the *Catechism* quotes, Mary "remained a virgin in conceiving her Son, a virgin in giving birth to him, a virgin in carrying him, a virgin in nursing him at her breast, always a virgin" (*CCC*, 510).

Her Divine Maternity

As we explained earlier, this dogma was defended and proclaimed at the Council of Ephesus in 431 and states that Mary can truly be called *Theotokos* or the Mother of God.

The Assumption of Mary into Heaven

Like the other dogmas, Mary's Assumption had long been held by Catholics through a tradition (oral, written, devotional, and liturgical) dating back to the event itself. To the great joy of the Church, however, it was solemnly defined on November 1, 1950, by Pope Pius XII when he stated in the encyclical

Munificentissimus Deus, "Mary, Immaculate Mother of God ever Virgin, after finishing the course of her life on earth, was taken up in body and soul to heavenly glory." If you read that definition over carefully, you can see that good Pope Pius managed to include all four Marian dogmas in one sentence!

* * *

And yet for all that, the beauty of this dear, humble hand-maiden of the Lord is that, in the words of our youngest Doctor, "she is more Mother than Queen." St. Thérèse of Lisieux, in words that anticipated and possibly inspired those of the Second Vatican Council, explained on her deathbed:

> For a sermon on the Blessed Virgin to please me and do me any good, I must see her real life, not her imagined life. I'm sure that her real life was very simple. . . . They should present her as imitable, bringing out her virtues, saying that she lived by faith just like ourselves, giving proofs of this from the Gospel, where we read: "And they did not understand the words which He spoke to them" [Luke 2:50]. And that other no less mysterious statement: "His father and mother marveled at what was said about Him" [Luke 2:33]. We know very well that the Blessed Virgin is Queen of heaven and earth, but she is more Mother than Queen. (*Last Conversations*, August 21, 1897)

So if you want to know what every Catholic should know about Mary, you have the basics now. If you want to know more about where to meet her, read on.

Chapter 10

Our Lady and Our Ladies

Her face was oval and of an incomparable grace, her eyes were blue, her voice, oh, so sweet!

— St. Bernadette Soubirous

In 1917 in the midst of the First World War, over a period of six months, Mary appeared to three shepherd children in Portugal. With each successive visit, the curious followed them and the crowds grew, until at last on October 13, 1917, there were seventy thousand people gathered in muddy fields, as close as they could get in the pouring rain to the three drenched children and the little holm oak tree over which they claimed The Lady appeared to them.

These crowds of tens of thousands included believers and atheists, as well as journalists and photographers from all the major Portuguese newspapers. The word had spread that The Lady had promised a miracle on this day, "a miracle for all to see and believe."

Sure enough, that day the seventy thousand saw the sun dance and spin in the sky, coloring everything—land, people, clouds—with gorgeous hues. Suddenly it seemed to leave its place and come hurtling toward them, causing many, including unbelievers, to fall onto their knees and yell out their sins, begging for mercy.

The sun did not hit or hurt them but returned to its place in the sky. The miracle had lasted about ten minutes. When it was over, the muddy ground and the drenched clothes of the witnesses were completely dry.

The journalists and photographers reported the miracle in all the major newspapers—secular, anti-Catholic, and openly atheistic newspapers, as well as religious ones. It was scientifically inexplicable and witnessed by tens of thousands, including some who were miles away and unaware that anything interesting had been predicted to happen. The contemporary documents—newspaper articles, photographs, interviews with witnesses—were many, and after more than one hundred years, they are still available in the public record.

The three shepherd children were a sister and brother, Jacinta and Francisco Marto, aged seven and nine, and their cousin Lucia dos Santos, aged ten. Jacinta and Francisco did not remain long on this earth, both falling ill in the influenza epidemic of 1918. Francisco was almost eleven when he died in 1919, and Jacinta was almost ten when she died a year later.

Indeed, Lucia, the eldest and the spokesperson of the group, had asked The Lady in the second visit whether they would go to heaven soon, and The Lady had answered, "I will take Jacinta and Francisco shortly; but you will stay here for some time to come. Jesus wants to use you to make me known and loved, to establish the devotion to my Immaculate Heart throughout the world." When Lucia seemed understandably distressed at being left alone, The Lady told her, "Don't lose heart. I will never forsake you. My Immaculate Heart will be your refuge and the way that will lead you to God."

As it turned out, Lucia stayed for what could arguably be called not merely "some time to come" but more like "a long time to come." She lived almost another ninety years, going finally to join her cousins in the company of Jesus and the beautiful Lady, His Mother and hers, when she was a month shy of her ninety-eighth birthday!

In the years after the apparitions of Our Lady of Fatima, Lucia did establish devotion to Mary's Immaculate Heart, and even more admirably, in my view, she kept a sense of humor while she did so. A cardinal who visited her when she was ninety-five recounted, "When I told her that I had spoken about Our Lady of Fatima in Lourdes, she remarked that it's a bad idea to confuse Our Ladies. Our Lady of Lourdes, she said, would surely take it amiss that I had spoken of Our Lady of Fatima on her turf!" (*The Last Secret of Fatima*). Good point, Lucia! And yet, what are we to do with all these Our Ladies?

The Assumption of Mary, the last dogma we mentioned in the previous chapter, puts Mary in a position where she has a good view of her children scattered across the globe. As St. Thérèse pointed out, "she is more Mother than Queen"; so it stands to reason that, seeing the difficulties, sufferings, and downright messes her children get themselves into, Our Lady's maternal instinct kicks in and she cannot stay away.

And so, here are some popular Our Ladies every Catholic should know. We have already spoken of Fatima. There Our Lady came to ask for penance and prayer in the early years of the bloodiest century the world has yet known. Sharing in the merciful vision of God, she knew long before we did what the years ahead would bring, and she invited the faithful to pray and sacrifice that calamities might be prevented and more hearts opened to the limitless love of the good God.

Our Lady of Guadalupe

In 1531, Mexico was in a bad way. Think human sacrifice. The first bishop of Mexico City was not gaining a foothold for the Truth in the morally barbaric civilization of the Aztecs, so he was saying a novena (nine days of prayer, in imitation of the Apostles' prayer with Our Lady in the upper room from Our Lord's Ascension to Pentecost) asking Mary to please help. She did.

She appeared to a poor indigenous Mexican named Juan Diego, whom she lovingly and tenderly called *Juanito* (little Juan) and Juan *Diegito*. On a cold December morning she gave him exquisite nonlocal, nonseasonal Castilian roses, which she herself arranged in his tilma (his cloak made of cactus fiber) for the bishop, along with her request that a chapel be built where she had appeared.

The bishop had heard from Juan Diego about Our Lady's request for a chapel in the previous days, but he had asked for a sign. When Juan returned with the miraculous roses, they may have been enough to convince the bishop, but we'll never know because there was more. When Juan dropped them from his tilma, the bishop and his retinue fell to their knees in awe. On Juan's tilma was a perfect likeness of the Lady who wanted a chapel: the Mother of God, come to answer the bishop's fervent prayers. He did build a chapel, which became a huge basilica. To this day, millions go there each year to see and admire Juan Diego's tilma, which continues to miraculously bear the image of Our Lady and equally miraculously continues to exist (a cactus fiber cloak is not usually a garment for the ages).

You can enjoy the other great gift of Our Lady to us through St. Juan Diego without traveling to Mexico City: the words of comfort she left us that never fail to console. Like her image on the tilma, they are meant for us all:

> Hear and let it penetrate your heart, my dear little one:
> Let nothing discourage you, nothing depress you.
> Let nothing alter your heart or your countenance.

Am I not here who am your Mother?
Are you not under my shadow and protection?
Am I not your fountain of life?
Are you not in the folds of my mantle?
In the crossing of my arms?
Is there anything else that you need?
Do not fear any illness or vexation, anxiety or pain.

Returning to the days of Juan Diego and the bishop, you will be glad to know that within a short time, millions of Aztecs converted to the Catholic Faith, abandoning human sacrifice and replacing it, happily, with the Holy Sacrifice of the Mass.

Our Lady of Lourdes

Three centuries later in another part of the world, Mary appeared eighteen times to an uneducated French girl who lived with her impoverished family in an abandoned jail considered too unhealthy for even the worst criminals. These apparitions took place between February 11 and July 16, 1858.

On one of her visits—the ninth, on the twenty-fifth of February—Our Lady told Bernadette to drink and wash from the spring. Seeing no spring and gestured away from the nearby river Gave, the girl obediently scratched at a wet patch of ground, inspiring laughter in the crowds gathered to witness her beautifully reverent praying of the Rosary with the Lady they could not see.

Bernadette's prayer during the apparitions was truly wondrous to behold. During one of the later visits, on April 7, the town doctor, who had been skeptical of the apparitions, noticed that while Bernadette prayed the Rosary, the flame of a candle she held was continuously burning one of her hands.

This went on for fifteen minutes. The doctor examined her after and reported, with awe, that not only had Bernadette felt nothing unusual during her ecstasy, but also her hand was unburned.

This day in February, however, the crowd's silence turned to mockery, and they dispersed after watching Bernadette smear her mouth with mud. So they didn't notice the trickle of a stream that began to flow. Nor were they witnesses to the first of so many miraculous cures that came next.

At dawn on March 1, Catherine Lapatie, her young children in tow, arrived at Lourdes, met Bernadette, and went with her to the grotto, where, by dipping her hand in water that had gathered in the little hollow by the spring, Catherine regained the use of two paralyzed fingers on her right hand.

Soon enough, though, the world knew about the miracles at Lourdes. These miracles, with the many ex-votos such as crutches and canes left by those healed, followed in the wake of Bernadette's simple, humble narrative, consistent no matter how many times she was asked to repeat it, no matter how tricky her questioners.

The final proof for Bernadette's bishop, however, like the tilma for the bishop in Mexico, was a gift of Our Lady, as beautiful as it was unexpected.

Bernadette was uneducated, but furthermore, she had a terrible time trying to learn her catechism to receive First Communion because she was, even in the face of the education offered, not the brightest bulb in the pack. Imagine, then, the bishop's surprise when Bernadette finally revealed the Lady's name. He had been hounding her to find it out, and Bernadette had, in obedience, repeatedly asked the Lady. Eventually the answer came. The Lady told her, in French (they were in France, after all), but moreover in Bernadette's own Gascon dialect, "I am the Immaculate Conception."

Poor Bernadette! She had no idea what this meant and had to repeat it over and over as she made her way to the bishop's house with the answer. The bishop could not help but believe Bernadette. He was well aware of her simplicity, and her ignorance coupled with this astonishing answer was proof of her truthfulness.

Pope Pius IX had defined the dogma of Mary's Immaculate Conception three and a half years before, but the news had not reached the likes of Bernadette in the abandoned jail in the small village high up in the Pyrenees. Not to mention Our Lady's interesting way of expressing her identity, for she did not say to Bernadette, "I am the one immaculately conceived," but "I am the Immaculate Conception." Some decades later in the first half of the twentieth century, this interesting formulation kept St. Maximilian Kolbe fascinated and seeking to discover its meaning throughout his entire life!

The Lady had asked that a chapel be built, and like the one she requested in Mexico, this church grew into a basilica visited by millions each year. The trickling spring grew into a torrent that supplies water in baths into which the sick are immersed for healing, although they are just as likely to be cured in the shadow of the Blessed Sacrament at the nightly processions when Our Lord, in the hands of the priests, blesses them.

Pilgrims can also wash themselves or fill vessels with the miraculous water channeled through a row of spigots beside the grotto where Our Lady appeared, but again, it is the sacraments that cleanse them. When I went to Lourdes in the summer of 1984, I was profoundly moved by the multitude of confessionals in the Basilica of the Immaculate Conception there—each confessional with a placard identifying the languages understood by the confessors. The priests, themselves pilgrims from all over the world, took turns offering the healing Sacrament of Reconciliation to those who came to Lourdes.

Wherever she appears, Our Lady is—as she has been since that moment when she said yes to the archangel's message—a mother. She is Jesus' Mother and ours, and just as she clothed and fed Jesus, so she wants to clothe and feed us.

Our Lady of Mount Carmel

She clothes us in the scapular, a pair of small brown wool squares connected by a cord and worn over the shoulders, a miniature version of garb worn in the Middle Ages and still worn today by religious—that is, those sisters, brothers, and priests belonging to religious orders. The Dominicans and Carmelites, for instance, wear scapulars, which in their case are large long garments, an extra layer of their habit, again worn over the shoulders and draping down over the body.

Mary gave the brown scapular to St. Simon Stock on July 16, 1251, in answer to his petition for her protection and help for the Carmelite Order, which had recently moved from the Holy Land to Europe. The scapular thus became her gift, a sacramental that, like a little sacrament, effects what it signifies—in this case maternal protection, signified by clothing.

Over the years, the scapular became smaller and its privileges extended to the universal Church. Since Mary's accompanying promise is that whoever dies wearing the scapular will not suffer the eternal fires of hell, understandably it has been a treasured devotion of the faithful over the centuries. The popes have encouraged its use, and Pope St. Pius X allowed that a scapular medal bearing the images of, on one side, Our Lady of Mount Carmel and, on the other, the Sacred Heart could be worn around the neck as a substitute for the wool scapular.

Children are often enrolled in the scapular confraternity and given their first scapular at their First Holy Communion. If you need a scapular, they are available at Catholic stores and over the Internet. Once you are enrolled, each replacement scapular does not need a new blessing. Its efficacy and holiness come from the blessing you retain in virtue of your original enrollment. If you have not yet been enrolled in the scapular, you can ask a priest to perform the simple ceremony, and if he doesn't have the proper prayers on hand, you can easily find them online.

* * *

In the Litany of Loreto in the last chapter of this book, you will discover many other titles of Our Lady. Each has its own history, meaning, and devotees. While it can be initially confusing to sort out all the Our Ladies (though heaven help us if we don't, Lucia might tease), there is, finally, only one Our Lady. She is the Mother of God and our Mother, too, and we couldn't be more blessed.

Chapter 11

Queen of the Angels

Recommend yourself to your Angel Guardian.... Remember that you are to be guided by your Angel like a blind man, who cannot see the dangers of the streets, and trusts entirely to the person who leads him.

— St. Aloysius Gonzaga

Our Lady is Queen of the Angels, and this is no mean feat. We are not surprised that God has raised Christ above the angels, for the Incarnate Word is the Second Person of the Trinity. Though He is true man, He is also true God. Our Lady, by contrast, is merely and purely human, and yet she, too, has been raised above the angels. This need not surprise us, for as has been said, as Mother of the King, she is by His side as Queen, and on account of her Assumption body and soul into heaven, she is entirely raised up in glory. Nonetheless, the more we know about the angels, the more we will be in awe of Our Lady's magnificent place above them, for the angels are much more than meets the eye.

When we recite the Nicene Creed at Mass every Sunday, we profess our belief in "One God, the Father almighty, maker of heaven and earth, of all things visible and invisible." What do we mean when we say He made heaven and invisible things? We are proclaiming the existence of the angels.

There are three primary reasons we should know about God's invisible creation, the angels. First, so that we will better understand the greatness of God through knowledge of His effects. Second, because we live in the midst of a spiritual battle, and it behooves us to know that we are fighting and who is helping us to fight. And third, because God has given each of us an angelic companion, a guardian angel who guides and guards us from birth until death, and it is absurd that we know and think so little about so very powerful and loving a friend.

What, then, are angels?

They are the beings that hold a place between God and man, and this place makes so much sense that the ancient pagan philosophers (Aristotle in particular), even without revelation, suspected their existence.

Angels are pure spirits, immortal beings with intelligence (far beyond ours, for they are not weighed down by matter) and free will. Like God, they have no bodies, but like men, they are creatures, and thus limited.

Henri-Marie Boudon, a French priest and ascetic writer of the seventeenth century, describes them thus:

> The angelic nature is a whole world of perfection in itself. And this at least we know, that angels are spiritual substances, incorruptible by nature, utterly separate from matter and entirely free from all those infirmities which compass us on every side. They are all brightness and beauty, and their loveliness surpasses all the united charms of earth. Their intelligence is godlike, says St. Thomas, for their knowledge extends to all truths of the natural order, as well as to a great number of the supernatural order. They know all the secrets of nature, and all that remains most hidden from the greatest minds that ever existed, is intimately known to them. They know without labor countless things at the same time and in an instant of time, unaccompanied with

doubt or obscurity. They do not make use of discourse like men, nor comprehend the things they know after our manner—that is by reasoning from one thing to another; they understand everything at a glance, and this is why they are styled emphatically, Intelligences. (*Devotion to the Holy Angels*)

The amazing thing about angels is—well, there are plenty of amazing things about angels. In one way, they are the most obvious and beautiful part of God's creation. Granted, they are immaterial and so usually invisible, and in that respect, you may rightly think they are not obvious. But as my husband says about men: "Pure spirits in matter—what a terrible idea!" Not that any of God's ideas are actually terrible, but this one surely came from love because it seems that, time and again, our matter does tend to lead our spirits in the wrong direction. Meanwhile, more fittingly, the angels are pure spirit, and thus spared our vicissitudes (except insofar as they witness them).

But because they are pure spirits, and yet limited (unlike God), here is the truly amazing thing: each angel is a species unto itself! And yet, I can give you the happy news that despite their multiplicity in number and, exactly equally, in species, the Church has managed through the attention and devotion of her theologians to classify the angels so that we may have a clearer understanding of them.

Like most of Church doctrine, the truth about angels is found in the Bible, but if you tried to find it for yourself from square one, as it were, you might be at it for centuries. Consequently, allowing Holy Mother Church to share her accumulated and divinely validated wisdom with us and then searching for the reflection of this truth in the Bible is a much faster method. Taking into account our weak minds, our penchant for error, and our limited life-on-earth spans, we highly recommend this sequence (Church first, then Bible).

Regarding the angels, theologians from Pseudo-Dyonisius to St. Thomas Aquinas, the Angelic Doctor (so called for his angelic purity, his angelic wisdom, and his unsurpassed explanation of the angels) have taught us that there are three hierarchies of angels, each containing three choirs. All the angels see God in His essence, but the three hierarchies see created things in different ways.

Within the hierarchies, the angels are ranked in choirs according to their offices, or job descriptions, and the actions they perform. Beginning from the top, the angels are as follows: closest to God, the Seraphim, Cherubim, and Thrones; next, the Dominations, Virtues, and Powers; and finally, nearest to us (though still far above us), the Principalities, Archangels, and Angels.

After their creation, the angels chose to follow God—or not—and because of their nature as pure spirits, their decision was irrevocable. As St. Peter explains, "God did not spare angels when they sinned, but cast them into hell and committed them to chains of gloomy darkness to be kept until the judgment" (2 Peter 2:4), and the early Church Father St. John Damascene confirms, "There is no repentance for the angels after their fall, just as there is no repentance for men after death" (*On the Orthodox Faith*, 2, 4).

St. John in the Book of Revelation describes, after his vision of Mary crowned with stars, the battle of the angels:

Now war arose in heaven, Michael and his angels fighting against the dragon. And the dragon and his angels fought back, but he was defeated, and there was no longer any place for them in heaven. And the great dragon was thrown down, that ancient serpent, who is called the devil and Satan, the deceiver of the whole world—he was thrown down to the earth, and his angels were thrown down with him. (Revelation 12:7–9)

Even non-angelic intellects such as ours can see that this Scripture passage contains both good news and bad news.

The good news is that the Archangel Michael and the other good angels defeated the devil (also called Lucifer or "light bearer" since he was one of the highest angels) and the rest of the bad angels who had rejected God. The bad news is that those fallen angels were thrown down to earth, where to this day they have a vested interest in ruining the plans of God for humankind. As we hear a few verses later, after his failure to corrupt or sidetrack Mary in any way, "Then the dragon became furious with the woman and went off to make war on the rest of her offspring, on those who keep the commandments of God and hold to the testimony of Jesus" (Revelation 12:17).

This is why we must know and appreciate the angels nearest to us, the guardian angels. In the bold and reassuring words of St. John Bosco, "When tempted, invoke your Angel. He is more eager to help you than you are to be helped! Ignore the devil and do not be afraid of him: he trembles and flees at the sight of your Guardian Angel."[1]

Our guardian angels—in company with all the angels of every hierarchy—constantly see the face of God. We know this from the advice of Our Lord: "See that you do not despise one of these little ones. For I tell you that in heaven their angels always see the face of my Father who is in heaven" (Matthew 18:10).

St. Thomas teaches us that every babe in the womb is watched over by his mother's guardian angel, but at birth, God sends each person his own angel to guide, enlighten, and protect him until death. All the angels came into existence at once at the beginning of creation, as St. Augustine explains, when God said, "'Let there be light,' and there was light"

---

1 Jill Haak Adels, *The Wisdom of the Saints* (New York: Oxford University Press, 1989), 23.

(Genesis 1:3). Since each person throughout all of human history has a unique angel as his guardian, we know there are at least as many angels as people who have ever existed and will ever exist—and that is only to count the minimum number in one of the nine choirs of angels!

For most of us, our angels remain invisible guides who constantly protect and inspire us, but without much gratitude or acknowledgment on our part. We can do our best, with their help, to change this sad state of affairs.

Many saints received the remarkable grace of seeing their angels, because angels can take on visible forms (as we know from various angelic visitations in the Bible), and these saints had special need or special appreciation of their heavenly companions. St. Francesca of Rome, St. Gemma Galgani, and St. Padre Pio, to take three examples, spent many years seeing and conversing with their guardian angels. And yet, as St. Angela of Foligno experienced, "So great was my joy in Him that I took no heed of looking at the angels and the saints, because all their goodness and all their beauty was from Him and in Him." The angels are not God, and yet for those of us who have not seen God, their resplendence and glory are blinding enough! St. Bridget of Sweden said, "If we saw an angel clearly, we should die of pleasure."

And yet these angels we usually don't see are at work daily by our sides. Let's do our best to remember them and thank them frequently, if only in the simple prayer put on our lips by Holy Mother Church:

Angel of God, my guardian dear,
To whom God's love commits me here,
Ever this day be at my side,
To light, to guard, to rule and guide.

Chapter 12

The Communion of Saints

Those from whom I receive the greatest consolations and encouragement are those whom I know to be dwelling in Paradise.

—St. Teresa of Jesus

In the Creed we say we believe in the Communion of Saints. Unlike the angels, the saints are not pure spirits, nor were they all created at once. They are, though it is sometimes hard to realize, mere mortals who have walked the earth before us and managed, by God's grace, to love Him with their whole hearts, and their neighbors as themselves.

When I was a young wife and a graduate student in philosophy, I was a teaching assistant to a group of undergraduates at the University of Notre Dame. I was a terrible teacher, but I had these kids for an hour each Friday, so when I found out I was pregnant, I shared the information with them. Anything to fill up our time together with something interesting. And then when I found out I was expecting a boy, I announced that too. These sweet, paradoxical eighteen-year-olds, who had complained to me about the pressure they felt from their high-achieving parents, heard my news and immediately blurted out as one, "What do you want him to be when he grows up?"

The answer burst forth from the bottom of my heart: "I want him to be a saint!" Just as quickly, one of the students, speaking for all, said, "That's great for when he's dead. But what do you want him to be when he's alive?"

I explained—whether they understood, I don't know—that becoming a saint is, actually, a project for this life, not something to vaguely intend after death. But how does one go about it? How do we take best advantage of the holy things (the sacraments, the sacramentals, the merits of Christ that the Church so abundantly offers us) and, like the saints, love God and one another successfully?

One of the gifts of the Second Vatican Council was its clear teaching on the universal call to sanctity—that is, that we are all called to be saints. This is not a new teaching but a faithful echo of Christ's invitation in the Gospel. Still, it is a teaching that needed reiteration because too often we think of the saints as those miracle workers or unstained, practically angelic men and women of old with whom we have nothing in common. Nothing could be further from the truth. In fact, we have in common with them what was most effective in making them saints—namely, the infinite riches of Christ. St. Paul says it very plainly at the beginning of his Letter to the Ephesians in a passage that is forever on the Church's lips in the Liturgy of the Hours: "Blessed be the God and Father of our Lord Jesus Christ, who has blessed us in Christ with every spiritual blessing in the heavenly places" (Ephesians 1:3).

Having all these spiritual blessings—above all the Holy Eucharist (that is, Christ Himself)—in common with the saints, though, we may still find ourselves wondering how in the world to become saints ourselves.

There is a modern saint who asked the same question. She found herself entirely weak and absurdly small in comparison with the great saints, but having carefully read the Gospels and knowing that we are all called to be saints, she begged God to show her an easy way that she, too, could become one. God answered her by showing her that the easiest way, as well as the most reliable, is the one Our Lord pointed out when His Apostles were asking (or rather making bets among themselves) who would be greatest in the kingdom of heaven.

In his homily at St. Thérèse of Lisieux's canonization, Pope Pius XI quoted Jesus in His response to the disciples: "Calling a child and setting him in their midst, He pronounced these memorable words: 'Amen, I say to you, unless you be converted and become as little children, you shall not enter into the Kingdom of Heaven.'" The pope then explained the secret of Thérèse's sanctity by recalling, "The new Saint Thérèse had learned thoroughly this teaching of the Gospels and had translated it into her daily life. Moreover she taught the way of spiritual childhood by word and example.... She set it forth clearly in all her writings, which have gone to the ends of the world." And finally, the Holy Father stated, "Therefore We nurse the hope today of seeing springing up in the souls of the faithful of Christ a burning desire of leading a life of spiritual childhood. That spirit consists in thinking and acting, under the influence of virtue, as a child feels and acts in the natural order."

Pope Pius XI's predecessor, Pope Benedict XV, had expressed a similar hope a few years earlier when he confessed in his speech on Thérèse's heroic virtues in 1921, "It is our special desire that the secret of her sanctity may be disclosed to all our children. The more the knowledge of this new heroine is spread abroad, the greater will be the number of her imitators giving glory to God by the practice of the virtues of spiritual childhood." That's great news that we have found the secret of sanctity lived by an actual canonized saint and endorsed by the popes, but what exactly is this secret? What is it about children that we are supposed to imitate? Precisely what is this easy way to sanctity that was the answer to St. Thérèse's prayers?

In the last months of the Little Flower's short life, one of her sisters asked our question, and Thérèse described her little way of becoming a saint:

> It is to recognize our nothingness, to expect everything from God as a little child expects everything from its father; it is to be disquieted about nothing, and not to be set on gaining our living....
>
> To be little is not attributing to oneself the virtues that one practices, believing oneself capable of anything, but to recognize that God places this treasure in the hands of His little child to be used when necessary; but it remains always God's treasure. Finally, it is not to become discouraged over one's faults, for children fail often, but they are too little to hurt themselves very much. (*Last Conversations*, August 6, 1897)

Hearkening back to my conversation with the undergraduates, I think they were making two understandable mistakes. First, they thought the only people who were saints were dead people, and second, if they did connect these seemingly dead saints in heaven to the people they had been on earth, my students still had the misconception that these saints were totally unlike themselves, because the saints had no faults in this life, but only virtues from infancy to old age.

What St. Thérèse did was to bring holiness and sanctification (becoming a saint) from the unattainable realm of "the perfect" and "the miracle workers" down to the level of children, which we all start life as and which we can admit, if we are honest, few of us progress far beyond no matter how long we live.

Thus her Little Way opens up the path to holiness for everyone, but Thérèse has more to teach us; there is another side to this coin. She knew, and she wants us to know, that because saints actually do come from among our ranks, once they are in heaven, they are all the more approachable.

Toward the end of Thérèse's earthly life, the seminarian who had become her spiritual brother was saddened by her impending death. He had trouble imagining how he could get along without their continued correspondence, and he also worried that once she really knew him in the light of the vision of God, she wouldn't love him anymore, imperfect sinner that he was. In her last letter, Thérèse wrote,

> I have to tell you that we don't understand Heaven in the same way. You think that, once I share in the justice and holiness of God, I won't be able to excuse your faults as I did when I was on earth. Are you then forgetting that I shall also share in the infinite mercy of the Lord? I believe that the Blessed in Heaven have great compassion for our miseries. They remember that when they were weak and mortal like us, they committed the same faults themselves and went through the same struggles, and their fraternal tenderness becomes still greater than it ever was on earth. It's on account of this that they never stop watching over us and praying for us. (*General Correspondence*, Letter 263, August 10, 1897)

The saints in heaven care about us a great deal and are, in Christ, our brothers and sisters. Some of these "Blessed in Heaven" are canonized, and some are not, but all are interested in us—often even before we are interested in them. Let this consoling doctrine remind you in times of loneliness that, truly, you are never alone. Besides the Blessed Trinity residing in your soul and the angel He has given to guard your ways, you are surrounded by a cloud of witnesses who not only know you but also love you.

To begin to know and love these saints who know and love you, a good starting place is with those whose names you share. These are your patron saints! If you frequent a church named after a saint, that saint is another good patron to discover. And then if there are statues of the saints in your parish church, these are another set of friends to learn more about. If you don't know who these statues represent, ask, or you may be able to puzzle out their identities with this clue: the Church has a rich history of iconography in which different symbols are used with different saints.

For instance, the statue of a bearded man holding a carpenter's square and a lily? St. Joseph (the lily is for purity). The statue of a nun holding a crucifix covered with roses? St. Thérèse of Lisieux. A tonsured man (his hair is a fringe around his head) in a brown robe holding a book with the baby Jesus sitting on it? St. Anthony of Padua. You will want to know him in particular because not only is he a Doctor of the Church, but he is also the patron of lost things, and who among us hasn't been desperate to find something we have lost?

As to the accusation some make that these statues promote idolatry, know that the Church has long appreciated images of the saints as reminders of our brothers and sisters in heaven, which inspire us not only to imitate them but also to ask their intercession with God, whose good friends they have proven to be. Since they are also our good friends, it's natural that we should think of them and ask their help.

Another ancient custom that may cause confusion is the veneration of the relics of the saints. These relics may be from their physical remains (called "first class"), items they used ("second class"), or items, usually pieces of cloth, touched to their remains ("third class"). The practice of honoring the holy things connected to a saint goes back to the time of Christ, and we can understand this practice by thinking of the devotion and honor we pay to the things (and the bodies) connected with our own beloved dead.

In the happiest of families, the dispersal of mom's rings among her children is not about who gets the most valuable but about having something dear that she wore, that one may wear it and remember her and, crazy as it might sound, feel closer to her and still connected to her. So, too, the loving care people take of their spouse's or child's grave, their desire to stay awhile and chat at the place of the remains, is natural and a testament to the physical connection we have with what is left by (or of) those who die, even when we know their souls are gone to eternal life.

When it comes to the saints, their remains have often been the instruments for miracles that God bestows on the faithful who venerate them. In some cases, the bodies of the saints have themselves been miracles, incorrupt in such a way that science can only verify the fact but not explain the mystery. And then there are saints' bodies, like St. Thérèse's, that after death are just as normally corrupted as ours will someday most likely be.

The Church has also traditionally named various saints as patrons in charge of particular needs, countries, professions, and so on. St. Joseph is the patron of fathers, carpenters, and a happy death; St. Jude Thaddeus (the Apostle) is the patron of desperate and impossible cases, and St. Rita of hopeless ones; St. Anthony, as mentioned, is the patron of lost things; St. Francis de Sales is the patron of writers; and the list goes on.

There are many excellent books about the saints, and many wonderful saints who have been converted by reading them. As St. Alphonsus de Liguori said, "The reading of the lives of the saints contributes greatly to infuse courage into the soul." Pope St. John Paul II used to keep the biographies of saints, the very ones he had canonized, in his bedroom so he could read them at night for encouragement and inspiration. May he, and all our brothers and sisters, pray for us, that we may someday be with them in the presence of God.

Chapter 13

How to Become a Saint

The science of the saints is to know the love of God.

— St. Alphonsus de Liguori

A few years ago I asked a holy ninety-something-year-old Jesuit priest friend what I should do to become a saint. His response to my question was a ready smile and the quick reply, "Oh, *you* can't become a saint!"

I wasn't sure whether to laugh or cry, until he followed up with the punch line: "*You* can't become a saint. Only Jesus can make you one!"

His timing was perfect, but the truth of his answer even more so. We cannot become saints, but surely Jesus can make us saints, and our part is merely to do our very poor best to cooperate. And then? We may never be canonized, but then again, stranger things have happened!

When the requests started coming in to the Lisieux Carmel that they should set the wheels in motion for Thérèse to be officially named a saint, the reactions of her sisters were really funny. They were not what we might expect regarding one who was to become such a huge star in the celestial firmament— "the greatest saint of modern times," according to Pope St. Pius X. One of the responses to the suggestion was, "What? Are we now to make every Carmelite nun a saint?" and her own blood sister Leonie, at the Visitation Convent in Caen, said, "Thérèse was nice. But a saint? Really?" I would love to know how Leonie is now taking the news of her own recent cause for canonization. I can almost hear her laughter.

Because, as we have already mentioned, the saints are, first and foremost, merely mortal like us. Really like us: they had to cut their fingernails and figure out what to eat. They had to make decisions about whether God wanted them to marry or become priests or religious. They were born into families where sometimes the relationships were strained and other times their dearest loved ones died all too soon.

St. Francis of Assisi loved a certain almond cookie that a noblewoman, Blessed Jacoba, made for him when he visited. He was known for his austerity; he loved Lady Poverty for Christ's sake, but when I think about his enjoyment of those almond cookies made out of charity just for him, I think of a certain homemade chocolate-chip cookie that a friend makes when I visit, out of charity for me, and I think sanctity is not necessarily as hard as we imagine!

Pope Benedict XVI gave a long series of Wednesday audiences on the saints, week after week talking about the great heroes of our Faith. He concluded on April 13, 2011, with a more general talk on holiness, but with quite specific particulars about how we, too, can become holy. He said,

> What is the essential? The essential means never leaving a Sunday without an encounter with the Risen Christ in the Eucharist; this is not an additional burden but is light for the whole week. It means never beginning and never ending a day without at least a brief contact with God. And, on the path of our life it means following the "signposts" that God has communicated to us in the Ten Commandments, interpreted with Christ, which are merely the explanation of what love is in specific situations. It seems to me that this is the true simplicity and greatness of

a life of holiness.... This is the true simplicity, greatness, and depth of Christian life, of being holy.

Despite the multitude of things every Catholic should know, our goal (union with Christ, which is holiness) is not that complicated. Pope Benedict has spelled out the exact particulars we are called to practice, and they make for a short list.

When we talk about becoming a saint, however, we can be talking about one of two things. First, there is our personal sanctification: our becoming ever more perfectly united to Our Lord, until such time as He takes us home to heaven to live with Him in eternal joy and glory. But second, we might be thinking about what it takes for a person who is in heaven to be glorified on earth, stamped by the Church with the official title of "Saint So and So."

Pope Benedict XVI gave us the answer to the first question, and it remains for us to consider the second: How does one become a canonized saint?

From the earliest days of Christianity, when one's friends and family were just as likely martyred as not, people revered, honored, and invoked those who had died—been killed—for Christ. They honored, too, those who had willingly confessed His name despite the danger of martyrdom.

While the Church, even in ancient times, investigated and confirmed the holiness of individuals to protect the faithful from confusion and error, for the most part the "process of sainthood" back then was one of popular acclaim. As the centuries passed, the process became more official, and around the year 1000, a consistent, formal series of steps were in place for the Church to assure the faithful that one of their own had made it safely home. In the twentieth century, Pope St. John Paul II oversaw the streamlining of the process. And so we can now answer that perennial question: How does one become a saint?

First and foremost, always start by getting to heaven, because the Church canonizes only those who are there. In fact, beatification (the step before canonization) is the Church's declaration that a person is already in heaven. The final step, canonization, is only the further declaration that God wants the Blessed (the beatified one) to be honored not only locally but also throughout the universal Church.

Here is how the whole official process works. A person lives a good life, a holy life, by the grace of God. So holy that those around him want, when the person dies, to ask for favors and help from their friend whom they are confident is with God, and they also want everyone else to know about this shining example of virtue.

The family and friends, and even those who know the holy one only by reputation, then petition not only the suspected saint in heaven but also the local bishop on earth. Their collective confidence, and the report of miracles, may just move the bishop to begin an investigation into the holiness of this popular and revered person. The bishop is the one who decides whether to open an official process, or Cause for Canonization, and if he does, the holy person in question is now a Servant of God.

The first phase of the Cause is the diocesan inquiry, also called the informative phase. An information-gathering investigation is made under a postulator and vice-postulator (both chosen by the petitioners), who are overseen by the bishop. The writings of the potential saint are gathered and examined, those who knew him are interviewed, and a study of his life is made. The goal is to gather all available evidence that will prove the person lived a life of heroic virtue or was martyred, had a reputation for holiness, and serves already as a role model and intercessor for the faithful. The gathered material is sent to Rome, and if approved, the Congregation for the Causes of Saints assigns a relator to write two *positios* on the prospective saint: one a biography presenting evidence and argument for heroic virtue, the other a presentation of the prospective saint's miracle(s).

The next title honoring the holy one is Venerable, a name given when heroic virtue is proven and approved. Heroic virtue is not just the virtue of a hero but a virtue beyond human power. How, then, is a person heroically virtuous if such virtue is by definition beyond his power? The very reason heroic virtue is a sign of a person's sanctity is because this virtue is infused by God and thus a sign of the person's transforming union with Him.

The most familiar and most dramatic part of the canonization process concerns the miracles. Whether or not a saint-in-the-making was known for miracles during his lifetime, the key to beatification and canonization is miracles obtained by his intercession after death, because such posthumous miracles attest to the person's proximity to God in heaven.

It is God who made everything and rules over creation. It is God who has power over the laws of nature. It is God, always and alone (if we want to speak carefully), who performs miracles. We speak loosely of saints performing miracles, and this is fine shorthand, as long as we remember that any power they have is borrowed—or better yet, is power over the heart of God, who delights to answer their fervent and confident petitions for us.

Consequently two things must be proved regarding the miracles for beatification and canonization: (1) that God truly worked a miracle (almost always some physical healing) and (2) that this miracle was granted through the intercession of the Servant of God or Venerable.

One of the changes Pope St. John Paul II implemented in the process was the reduction of miracles needed for a person to be beatified (from two to one) and canonized (again from two to one). In the case of martyrdom, it has been the recent tradition, even before the changes instituted in 1983, that no miracle is needed for beatification since martyrdom itself is a convincing one.

Far from rubber-stamping miracles right and left, the Church has a careful procedure to authenticate both that a miracle occurred—medical doctors must investigate physical healings, the "before and after" medical records, the person healed, and so on—and that it occurred through this particular holy one's intercession.

A friend of mine gravely ill with cancer had a devotion to a Servant of God and prayed that, if God willed, she would be healed through that holy one's intercession. God did not so will, preferring to take my friend home to Himself quickly, but first my friend enjoyed working with a local priest in spreading the request that others would pray to this particular Servant of God so that, if she were healed, the records might be sent to Rome with accompanying evidence of *this* saint's intercession.

In the cases where God grants a miracle, after medical experts and theologians scrutinize the evidence and confirm it, the holy one is ready for beatification. With this step, the Church announces that the Blessed is in heaven and the faithful may imitate, invoke, and publicly honor him, but this honor is usually limited to the religious order to which the Blessed belonged or the region in which he lived.

Sometimes the Cause stops there. No more is requested, and no more is done. Other times, miracles occurring after the beatification indicate that God wants this Blessed raised even higher, for universal veneration by, imitation by, and friendship with all the faithful. The Church requires that the miracle for canonization occur after the beatification precisely to give God a chance to show His desire for such worldwide acclamation.

My favorite example of God's desire to so glorify one of His faithful children occurred on April 29, 1923, the day

Pope Pius XI beatified Sister Thérèse of the Child Jesus and she became Blessed Thérèse. Soon after, the Carmel in Lisieux received letters from all over attesting to thirty miracles granted through Thérèse's intercession that very day. God was apparently in a hurry!

The saints love us. They want us to join them with God in heaven. They want, in a word, for us to become saints too. Whether or not we share the official title with them, we will have our own commemorative day in the Church's calendar on the first of November. This is the Feast of All Saints, the day on which the Church remembers, honors, and asks the intercession of not just the canonized and beatified but every soul, however hidden, who has made it safely into the presence of God. In the next chapter, we'll take a look at this calendar and page through the Church's liturgical year, that we might better celebrate her fasts and feasts and so become saints ourselves.

Chapter 14

The Liturgical Year

Beginning with the Easter Triduum as its source of light ... the Resurrection fills the whole liturgical year with its brilliance. Gradually, on either side of this source, the year is transfigured by the liturgy.

— *Catechism of the Catholic Church*

Just as our family and friends help us to celebrate our birthdays, so, too, the Church helps us to celebrate the birthdays of the saints. Only, in the case of the saints, we usually skip their earthly birthdays and celebrate instead their birthdays into heaven.

Similarly, just as the calendar year helps us mark the seasons of fall, winter, spring, and summer, so, too, the Church calendar or liturgical year helps us mark the seasons of Advent, Christmas, Lent, and Easter.

The greatest feast in the liturgical year is Easter, when Our Lord rose from the dead on the third day after His Passion, Crucifixion, and Death. When I was a girl, I got into an argument with one of my teachers when I insisted that Christmas was the greatest feast of the year. While I now understand why she insisted on Easter, I can't blame my nine-year-old self for arguing that He couldn't have died to save us if He hadn't first been born, and besides, how could a day with presents for everyone not be the best of the best?

To prevent unnecessary conflicts like this, the Church has an established hierarchy of ranks for her feasts, from optional memorials (the lowest), up through feasts, all the way to solemnities of the Lord (highest). In honor of Easter, every Sunday of the year is a "little Easter" and a solemnity of the Lord. This is why, in obedience to the third commandment and the first precept of the Church, we go to Mass every Sunday. And in between Sundays? Often we find days marked as memorials of the saints, and on these days we celebrate too.

Have you ever heard the expression "Hunger is the best sauce"? The Church in her maternal wisdom knows this to be true, and she knows, too, that if we are always feasting, we won't appreciate what we have been given. For this and other reasons, she gives us fasts as well as feasts, and the order is always fast first, then feast.

If we take a look at the bigger picture (think weeks rather than days), we find that the Church gives us not only days of fasting and feasting but also whole seasons. Given our flighty natures, our distractions, and our forgetfulness, the Church has kindly provided more than merely a moment thinking of this and a moment tasting that.

Instead, to give us something to chew on and a sustained period of reflection, starting around the beginning of December each year she offers us four weeks of Advent, a time of gentle penance and growing anticipation for a triple coming: first, Christ's birth (or Nativity) in the stable at Bethlehem; second, His meeting with each of us at our deaths; and third, His return in triumph at the end of time.

Christmas, on which we celebrate the Nativity of our Savior, is not merely a day but begins with the day of His birth on December 25 and extends for twelve days (the famous "Twelve Days of Christmas") to Epiphany, when the three wise men worshipped the Holy Infant.

After the Second Vatican Council, the Church revised her liturgical calendar to simplify it (as she has done many times in the past), but when she later reintroduced the old Mass in the Extraordinary Form, the old calendar was also revived. Consequently, there is a distinction here to be made. In the new calendar, Christmas as a season lasts a few weeks after the Feast of Epiphany, while in the old calendar, following the Feast of Epiphany is the season of Epiphany. Either way, again the Church gives us time to savor our spiritual feast, prolonging our Christmas joy and our meditation on this great mystery.

Next, sometime in February or March (depending on the lunar calendar and related Jewish feast of Passover), comes Ash Wednesday, a day of fasting and abstinence that ushers in our major season of penance, the forty days of Lent. During Lent we accompany Christ on His forty-day fast in the desert and prepare our hearts for His Passion, Death, and Resurrection in Holy Week.

Holy Week, in the sixth week of Lent, follows Palm Sunday. The Church drapes purple cloth over the statues and crucifixes in her churches, and the week of Our Lord's great suffering is upon us. We begin the week with the welcome Jesus received in Jerusalem, with children waving palm branches and singing, "Hosanna in the highest, blessed is He who comes in the name of the Lord!" Too soon, though, we descend with Christ into His week of sorrow.

On Spy Wednesday, the Mass readings remind us of Judas's betrayal. On Holy Thursday, in the morning the bishop gathers the priests of his diocese for the Chrism Mass, during which he blesses all the holy oils to be used in the sacraments for the next year.

On Holy Thursday night, the Easter Triduum of the Passion and Resurrection of the Lord begins with the Mass of the

Lord's Supper. We gather for a reenactment of Jesus' washing the Apostles' feet, we celebrate the first Mass with Him, and we follow the priest as he leads Jesus in the Blessed Sacrament to an altar of repose, signifying His retreat to the Garden of Gethsemane, where He began His Passion, suffering in agony for us and sweating blood.

Good Friday is the saddest day of the year. The Blessed Sacrament is not in the tabernacle, the red sanctuary lamp does not glow, and the holy water fonts are empty. When entering church on Good Friday, we don't bless ourselves with holy water, nor do we genuflect when we enter a pew, for there is no Jesus before us in the tabernacle, no God there before whom we bend our knee. Instead, we make a simple bow to the altar, in reverence for the Sacrifice that takes place upon it.

Good Friday is a perfect time (as is Holy Saturday) to make our Lenten Confession if we haven't done so yet or want (or need) to do so again, that our souls might be their very purest to receive Jesus on Easter. But meanwhile, the church is silent.

On Good Friday the Church offers no Mass, for we are entering into the one sacrifice occurring this day for all time on Calvary, where Jesus is crucified for us. Instead of Mass, we have a Celebration of the Lord's Passion, in which the Gospel of the Passion is read. We venerate the Cross, filing up to the front of the church as if we were going to receive Holy Communion but instead taking our turn to kiss Jesus on the Cross. We pray a long list of petitions for everyone in need of our prayers, from the pope down through the Church's ranks and out her doors to those of other religions and none, government officials, and all in need of our prayers. Finally, the priests, deacons, and altar servers prepare the altar and bring the Blessed Sacrament from the sacristy, where it has been kept. We receive Our Savior in Communion, and our union with His suffering is complete.

Holy Saturday is the day when Jesus descends to the dead and announces to them His victory. It is a solemn and quiet day, a day to keep company with our Mother Mary, who stood at the foot of His Cross and was given to us as our Mother yesterday. She waits today, and we wait with her.

And then, the Easter Vigil, the most splendid night of the year, the feast that follows the fast, the victory that follows the Cross. This is the night on which the Easter candle, representing Christ, is lit and lights every other candle in the church. It is the night on which we review our salvation history in a panoply of readings from the Old and New Testaments. It is also the night on which converts are received into the Church through the Sacraments of Baptism and Confirmation.

It is a night of great joy—the greatest we may know this side of the grave and our own victories, in Christ, over death. With this night, we enter Easter, and this season does not last merely four weeks, like Advent, nor six weeks, like the Lent that precedes it, but seven weeks—beginning with an octave (eight days) that is all one long solemnity, culminating in the Feast of Divine Mercy. I must admit, my teacher was right, and the liturgical calendar educates us and bears this out: there is no question that Easter is the solemnity of solemnities!

Forty days after His Resurrection, Jesus ascended into heaven, and so, near the end of the seven weeks of Easter, we celebrate the Ascension of the Lord. This is the time when the Church really began to pray, learning to pray from Our Lady, who waited in the Cenacle (the upper room) with the disciples, as the Lord had instructed them before His Ascension. We wait again with them, praying the novena (nine day) prayer to the Holy Spirit, who then descends upon them and us at Pentecost.

And then what? Following the octave of Pentecost, or its season (depending if you are looking at the new or old calendar), what about the remaining days of the year—those days between seasons and the great solemnities to which these seasons lead?

The Church is never boring. If, like children sometimes do, we complain of boredom, our problem, like theirs, is not that the world around us is boring but that we are failing to enter into it with a proper spirit of wonder. For looking more closely we see, dotted across the landscape of the liturgical year, feasts like flowers and other feasts like stars, beautifying and lighting up the cycle of the year as it passes and repasses in a whirl of grace.

Some of these feasts are solemnities in their own right, celebrating and honoring the major moments in the life of Our Lord, the privileges of Our Lady, and the most remarkable and universal of the saints. The most important of these solemnities are often holy days of obligation (these are in bold below), on which we are obligated to attend Mass, but check your local church calendar because these can vary by country and even by diocese.

The principal solemnities are as follows, starting from the beginning of the Church year, which begins with Advent:

December 8: Immaculate Conception of Mary
December 25: Nativity of the Lord (Christmas)
January 1: Solemnity of Mary the Mother of God
January 6: Epiphany (often transferred to the following Sunday)
March 25: Annunciation to Mary and Incarnation of the Lord (Not a holy day of obligation in the United States, this solemnity celebrates, nine months before Christmas, when the Word was made flesh in the Virgin's womb; when March 25 occurs in Holy Week or Easter Week, this solemnity is transferred to the Monday after the Octave of Easter.)

Easter

Ascension Thursday (sometimes transferred to the following Sunday)

Pentecost Sunday

August 15: Assumption of the Blessed Virgin Mary

November 1: Solemnity of All Saints

It is fitting that we end this list with the Feast of All Saints on November 1 because while there are many other solemnities and feasts we have not mentioned, there is one last day that charity obliges us to note. The day after we celebrate all the saints in heaven, we pray for those who may have not yet made it there. November 2 is All Souls' Day, and on this day we are invited into a month-long remembrance of the dead who are uncanonized. Many may still be in purgatory and thus in need of our prayers. We will say more about these souls in a later chapter because scarcely enough can be said about our special bond with them.

One last interesting fact about the liturgical year: assigned to the feasts and seasons are various liturgical colors. Red denotes martyrdom and the Holy Spirit. Purple is the color of sorrow and penance. White is the color of purity and sanctity. Black is the color of mourning. Green, interestingly, shows up during the new calendar's weeks of Ordinary Time, so named because we count these weeks between seasons with ordinal numbers, beginning with the First Week of Ordinary Time and going on into the Thirty-Fourth Week, when we complete the year with the Solemnity of Christ the King (which is the last Sunday in October in the old calendar; the last Sunday before Advent in the new calendar).

And there you have it—a year without parallel, so jam-packed with fasts, feasts, and seasons. Each of them is worthy of a lifetime of meditation, and before you know it, we will have made it through all the years granted us, however many or few, and celebrate these same feasts in all their glorious splendor in heaven.

Meanwhile, we walk from day to day in obedience to those whom God in His providence has set over us as leaders of the Church. With them, we carry the treasures of our Faith along well-worn paths, toward our common goal. In the next part of this book, we will consider our leaders, examine our heritage, and take a final glance at what awaits us.

Chapter 15

Popes, Bishops, and Ecumenical Councils

There is one God and one Christ, and one Church, and one Chair founded on Peter by the word of the Lord.

—St. Cyprian

At the beginning of this book we made a distinction between "the Church" and "the church." At that early juncture I was concerned with telling as much as I could in a short book about what one might expect to find and do in a Catholic church. Now, having also considered our Mother Mary and our brothers and sisters, the saints, we must take a closer look at the other important personages we find in the Catholic Church. In particular we will look at those associated with the leadership of what may be called—to use an ugly word that almost has no place here—the institution of the Church.

We can reconcile ourselves to the Church occasionally being called an institution because she was, from her own beginning, instituted by Christ. But having made that linguistic concession, let's remember that the Church is the Mystical Body of Christ and thus, like her Head, divine as well as human.

When Jesus began His public ministry, many were attracted to Him and followed Him. In the Gospel we read of the first encounters between Jesus and several of the Apostles, but we also find confirmation that He did not merely take anyone who came, nor allow them to figure out their own hierarchy. St. Luke tells us quite specifically in the sixth chapter of his Gospel that Jesus called the twelve Apostles out of His many disciples (the much larger group of His followers) only after long prayer.

Among those Jesus chose, there was one who exhibited exceptional leadership abilities. He was strong-minded, determined, and articulate—or, in other words, impetuous, stubborn, and extremely outspoken. He was a man of passion, an all-or-nothing personality. After denying Christ three times, he wept, but with Jesus' forgiveness he threw himself all the more enthusiastically into his mission. This was Simon, whom Jesus named Peter.

As St. Matthew, who was there when it happened, recounts for us, one day Jesus asked His disciples, "Who do people say that the Son of Man is?" (Matthew 16:13). He got a variety of answers but then focused the question: "But who do *you* say that I am?" (Matthew 16:15, emphasis added).

Simon didn't miss a beat. "You are the Christ, the Son of the living God." The other Apostles and disciples may have been rolling their eyes. There goes Peter again—he always has an answer! But Jesus, knowing everything, knew this was not simply Peter's personality asserting itself again. Far from it. And so, the Savior responded,

> Blessed are you, Simon Bar-Jonah! For flesh and blood has not revealed this to you, but my Father who is in heaven. And I tell you, you are Peter and on this rock I will build my church, and the gates of hell shall not prevail against it. I will give you the keys of the kingdom of heaven, and whatever you bind on earth shall be bound in heaven, and whatever you loose on earth shall be loosed in heaven. (Matthew 16:17–19)

Then again, after His Resurrection, Jesus confirmed Peter's role with a threefold commission that paralleled Peter's three-fold betrayal on Holy Thursday night. St. John the Apostle, in another eyewitness account, reports that after breakfast on the beach along the shore of the Sea of Tiberius, Jesus thrice asked Peter if he loved Him, and Peter responded each time, "Yes, Lord, you know that I love you." Jesus' response was, in turn: "Feed my lambs," and then, "Tend my sheep," and finally, "Feed my sheep" (John 21:15–17).

In these events, the Church has always seen, heard, and believed in God's choice of Peter as the first Vicar of Christ— that is, "the Pope, visible head of the Church on earth, acting for and in the place of Christ and possessing supreme ecclesiastical authority in the Catholic Church," as Servant of God Fr. John Hardon so clearly expressed it.[1]

Most Catholics are aware of the Second Vatican Council, a meeting of the bishops of the world in Rome, held intermittently between 1962 and 1965. What is less commonly known is that this ecumenical, or universal, council was a reconvening or continuation of the First Vatican Council, which took place in Rome a hundred years earlier, from 1869 to 1870, when eight hundred bishops were summoned there by Blessed Pius IX. The First Vatican Council was never completed because troops came and occupied Rome between sessions, but in the short time it met, the Council Fathers issued the important doctrinal constitution *Pastor Aeternus* (The Eternal Pastor), which clarified Church teaching on the papacy.

This beautiful document begins, "We teach and declare that, according to the gospel evidence, a primacy of jurisdiction over the whole Church of God was immediately and directly promised to the blessed apostle Peter and conferred on him by Christ the Lord." *Pastor Aeternus* goes on to confirm that

---

1 John J. Hardon, S.J., *Pocket Catholic Dictionary* (New York: Image Books, 1985), 451.

the pope as the true successor of Peter has full and supreme power of jurisdiction over the whole Church and that this primacy includes his teaching office, to which Christ added papal infallibility—that is, the guarantee that the pope does not err when he teaches definitively on faith and morals. The Council Fathers wrote,

> Therefore, faithfully adhering to the tradition received from the beginning of the Christian faith, to the glory of God our Savior, for the exaltation of the Catholic religion and for the salvation of the Christian people, with the approval of the Sacred Council, we teach and define as a divinely revealed dogma that when the Roman Pontiff speaks *ex cathedra*, that is, when, acting in the office of shepherd and teacher of all Christians, he defines, by virtue of his supreme apostolic authority, a doctrine concerning faith or morals to be held by the universal Church, he possesses, by the divine assistance promised to him in blessed Peter, that infallibility which the divine Redeemer willed His Church to enjoy in defining doctrine concerning faith or morals. (4:9)

If you ever find yourself immersed in the pages of history or the vicissitudes of the present papacy and worry about just exactly what to make of the Holy Father and the conclave of cardinals who elected him, here is another passage from *Pastor Aeternus* that you might find helpful, for its truth rests not only on the strength of its own conciliar weight but also on quotes from the Council of Ephesus and Pope St. Leo the Great:

> For "no one can be in doubt, indeed it was known in every age that the holy and most blessed Peter, prince and head of the apostles, the pillar of faith and the foundation of the Catholic Church, received the keys of the kingdom from our Lord Jesus Christ, the savior and redeemer of the human race, and that to this day and for ever he lives" and presides and

"exercises judgment in his successors" the bishops of the Holy Roman See, which he founded and consecrated with his blood. Therefore whoever succeeds to the chair of Peter obtains by the institution of Christ Himself, the primacy of Peter over the whole Church. "So what the truth has ordained stands firm, and blessed Peter perseveres in the rock-like strength he was granted, and does not abandon that guidance of the Church which he once received." (2:2–3)

St. Catherine of Siena, a third-order Dominican, lived in the fourteenth century during a time when many people wondered what God was thinking in His choice of popes. In those days the choice looked, due to political intrigue, much more like the machinations of men than a gift of God. St. Catherine didn't let this bother her. She placed her trust in God and knew that, whatever happened, He would take care of everything. Meanwhile, she had a unique mission: to bring Pope Gregory XI back to the papal residence in Rome from Avignon, France, where the popes had been living for sixty-seven years. She achieved God's task for her. The papacy was restored to Rome, and amid the myriad trials involved, Catherine never once forgot that the Church is Christ's Bride, and the pope is "the sweet Christ on earth."

Another of the pope's titles is "Servant of the servants of God," and yet another is "Bishop of Rome." Like Peter, he is the leader of his brethren, the other bishops, who take the place of the other Apostles. But as Christ his Master demonstrated when He washed their feet at the Last Supper, the pope, even more than the other bishops, is called to humbly serve.

This is great news about the primacy of Peter and his successors, but what about the other Apostles and their successors, the bishops?

Judas Iscariot had betrayed Jesus and afterward hung himself in despair. Thus after Jesus' Resurrection, Ascension, and the subsequent descent of the Holy Spirit on Pentecost, the remaining eleven Apostles chose, by lot, St. Matthias to join them and complete again their perfect fulfillment of the twelve tribes of Israel. Because Israel is a prototype of the Church, it is fitting that just as Israel had twelve leaders, so does the Church, and God often points out in the Scriptures the significant connection between these two groups of twelve men.

In the Book of Revelation, the Apostle John describes for us his vision of the Church, "the Bride, the wife of the Lamb," the holy city, the New Jerusalem. He saw it

> coming down out of heaven from God, having the glory of God, its radiance like a most rare jewel, like a jasper, clear as crystal. It has a great high wall, with twelve gates, and at the gates twelve angels, and on the gates the names of the twelve tribes of the sons of Israel were inscribed.... And the wall of the city had twelve foundations, and on them were the twelve names of the twelve apostles of the Lamb. (Revelation 21:9–12, 14)

Here we see with St. John the primacy of the twelve Apostles, who form the foundation of the Church.

St. Paul uses the same language—because the reality is the same—in his Letter to the Ephesians when he writes,

> So then you are no longer strangers and aliens, but you are fellow citizens with the saints and members of the household of God, built on the foundation of the apostles and prophets, Christ Jesus himself being the cornerstone, in whom the whole structure, being joined together, grows into a holy temple in the Lord. In him you also are being built together into a dwelling place for God by the Spirit. (Ephesians 2:19–22)

The document *Dei Verbum,* from the Second Vatican Council, explains what happened next, after that first foundation of the Apostles: "In order that the full and living Gospel might always be preserved in the Church the apostles left bishops as their successors. They gave them 'their own position of teaching authority'" (no. 7). In this way the faithful have never been left fatherless, never left without a divinely sanctioned set of teachers.

Vatican Council II also gave us a dogmatic constitution on the Church called *Lumen Gentium* (Light of Nations), which expresses with admirable clarity the bishops' share in the Apostles' and Peter's prerogatives:

> Although the individual bishops do not enjoy the prerogative of infallibility, they nevertheless proclaim Christ's doctrine infallibly whenever, even though dispersed through the world, but still maintaining the bond of communion among themselves and with the successor of Peter, and authentically teaching matters of faith and morals, they are in agreement on one position as definitely to be held. This is even more clearly verified when, gathered together in an ecumenical council, they are teachers and judges of faith and morals for the universal Church, whose definitions must be adhered to with the submission of faith. (nos. 40, 41)

This union of the bishops with the pope is sometimes called the Magisterium, by which is meant the teaching office of the Church. Whether in an ecumenical council or in the day-to-day teaching of the Church throughout the world, when the bishops are in union with the pope and one another and they present something as definitive, it is infallible.

So what is an ecumenical council? Sometimes also called a general council, it is a meeting of the bishops of the world for the purpose of responding to confusion in the Church, or affirming Church teachings, or addressing questions of faith and morals, or reforming. Although the first eight councils were called by emperors, with the Holy Father mostly sending legates (representatives) to meet with the bishops, *Lumen Gentium* explains that a council is not ecumenical unless it is confirmed or accepted as such by the pope, whose prerogative it is to convoke, preside over, and confirm such councils (no. 22).

There have been twenty-one ecumenical councils to date. The first eight were held in the East, in what is now Turkey; some of them have very familiar names: Nicaea, Constantinople, Ephesus, Chalcedon. The more recent thirteen have been in the West (in Europe), and some of these have familiar names as well: the Lateran Councils, the Council of Trent, and Vatican Councils I and II. You will find a full list of the ecumenical councils in the last chapter of this book.

The final way the successors of Peter speak to us is through their written documents. These have varying degrees of importance and authority, from encyclical letters to apostolic exhortations. In this age of ubiquitous media and frequent papal interviews, one helpful way to gauge the degree of authority with which the pope speaks on any particular occasion is by measuring the degree of formality with which he speaks. It is not hard to see that a truly formal proclamation will be at the other end of the spectrum from a casual airplane chat. Traditionally, encyclicals are proposed for more serious examinations of doctrine, while apostolic exhortations are just that: encouragement for the faithful.

On a practical note, if you are in the company of a bishop and are introduced to him, you address him as "Your Excellency." It has been a time-honored custom to kiss the bishop's episcopal ring in acknowledgment of his office, and you may wish to do so, but many bishops are uncomfortable with this act of devotion, so let the Holy Spirit be your guide.

As for the red-hatted cardinals, if you ever get to meet one, address him as "Your Eminence." Cardinals are named by the pope, and their job is to act as his principal counselors, aid in the governance of the Church throughout the world, and ultimately meet in conclave (a private meeting) after the pope dies in order to elect his successor, almost always from their own number. The cardinals pray to the Holy Spirit to guide them; from their inspired votes—mixed up, no doubt, with human free choice—comes the new pope.

Christ did not leave us without a teacher. We have the Church, and she speaks to us through the successors of Peter and the Apostles. Thankfully, as St. Ambrose expressed it, "The Church of the Lord is built upon the rock of the apostles among countless dangers in the world; it therefore remains unmoved."

Chapter 16

The Priesthood and Religious Life

Oh, how great is the priest! The priest will only be understood in heaven. Were he understood on earth, people would die, not of fear, but of love.

—St. John Vianney

If the end of the world as we know it were imminent and books (including this one) about to poof out of existence, I would want you to read and learn one sentence by heart, and then I could rest assured that you, as a Catholic, knew what you absolutely needed to know. Ready?

What every Catholic should know is that the Blessed Sacrament, the Holy Eucharist, is truly the Body and Blood, Soul and Divinity, of Jesus Christ and that the Catholic priesthood is holy and wondrous far beyond our ability to comprehend because the priest, *in persona Christi*, is the only one who can bring this Blessed Sacrament into being on our altars.

That seems too much to commit to memory, especially right before the end of the world as we know it, so let us sum up more concisely: *The consecrated host is God, and the priest is the only one who can consecrate the host.*

No wonder, then, that St. John Vianney, the patron saint of parish priests, said, "If priests are saints, what good they are able to do! But whatever they are, never speak against them." That's a tall order in our day, when many priests have been far from saints, and yet St. John Chrysostom, too, explains, "The most high and infinitely good God has not granted to angels the power with which He has invested priests."

St. John Chrysostom lived in the fourth century, and St. John Vianney in the nineteenth. They both were well aware of priests who lived badly and were blots on the moral landscape as well as a discredit to the priesthood. Yet both of these saints were bold and unflinching in their defense of the priesthood and their respect for priests. Why?

At the Last Supper the night before He died, Jesus gave His Body, Blood, Soul, and Divinity under the appearance of bread and wine—that is, He gave Himself in the Holy Eucharist—to the Apostles, whom He would be sending out to the ends of the earth with His message and mission. And when He said, "Do this in remembrance of me," He gave them the power of the priesthood by which they and all those who succeeded them would bring Him again into our midst in the Holy Sacrifice of the Mass.

On the day of His Resurrection, Jesus gave these same Apostles the power to forgive sins (in the Sacrament of Confession) when, as St. John the Evangelist tells us, "He breathed on them and said to them, 'Receive the Holy Spirit. If you forgive the sins of any, they are forgiven them; if you withhold forgiveness from any, it is withheld'" (John 20:22–23).

We see in these two events some of the priestly powers Christ gave His Apostles, but what, then, is a priest? What exactly is the priesthood?

In the words of the Jesuit Servant of God Fr. John Hardon,

> The priesthood is simultaneously four things: it is a sacrament of the new law instituted by Christ; it is a state of life to which some men are called by a special vocation from God; it is an institution without which there would be no Christianity on earth today; and it is a ministry of the Catholic Church by

which Christ continues His own priestly work of saving and sanctifying the souls for whom He shed His blood on Calvary.

If you remember our opening story about the Japanese Catholics who kept the Faith for hundreds of years without priests and without the Blessed Sacrament, you may wonder why Fr. Hardon claims that without the priesthood there would be no Christianity today. His point is not in contradiction to the history of the Church in Japan but rather highlights what an astounding miracle it was that the Japanese converted by St. Francis Xavier could keep the Faith without these normally necessary things: Jesus in the Holy Eucharist and the priests who bring Him to us through the transubstantiation that takes place in the Holy Sacrifice of the Mass.

Just as a physical miracle sometimes occurs by the continuous transcendence of grace over nature—such as in documented cases where a blind person miraculously healed can now see but the organic problem that caused the former blindness, such as a detached retina, still persists—similarly the perduring faith of the Japanese during those bleak centuries without the priesthood in Japan and thus without Jesus in the Eucharist ought to put us in awe of God's goodness and power.

Normally, we desperately need the daily fulfillment of Our Lord's last promise before His Ascension into heaven: "And behold, I am with you always, to the end of the age" (Matthew 28:20)—that is, His Real Presence remaining among us, that daily bread for which we pray in the Our Father. And this continuous Real Presence is possible only through the ministry of His priests. That is why Fr. Hardon, a master catechist and teacher of catechists, said on many occasions that Christianity could not survive without the priesthood.

I have been to Sunday Mass frequently with a holy Irish priest who leads the Nicene Creed in a marvelous way. He never says it at the same pace, which forces the rest of us, trying to keep up with him, to think about what we are proclaiming from beginning to end. But when he gets to one crucial line, Father goes so slowly that, no matter what else the congregation has missed, we don't miss this: "I believe in one ... holy ... catholic ... apostolic Church."

These are the four marks of the Church. We have touched on her holiness in our discussion of the Communion of Saints. We implied the unity or oneness of the Church when we talked in the previous chapter about the pope and the bishops in union with him, and we will address unity again in the next chapter. As for "catholic" as a mark of the Church, that simply points out her universality. The Apostles did, according to Christ's command, take His teaching and His sacraments to the ends of the earth, and they still do in the missions of today.

What concerns us now is this final mark: apostolic. Its meaning is simple but crucial, and every Catholic should understand it because it is central to the very existence and continuation of our Faith. "Apostolic" when applied to the Church means there is a direct line of succession from the Apostles, the first priests—who in fact were the first bishops too—and every Catholic priest since. Or to look at it from the other direction, every Catholic priest has a sort of bloodline, only in this case a grace-line, leading from his priesthood through the bishop who ordained him (for only bishops have the power to ordain other priests) to the bishop who ordained him, and so on, all the way back to the first bishops, the original Apostles given this power on Holy Thursday by Christ Our Lord Himself.

Returning to Fr. Hardon's fourfold explanation of the priesthood, we can summarize as follows:

1. The priesthood is a sacrament of the new law instituted by Christ.

2. It is a state of life to which some men are called by a special vocation from God.
3. It is an institution without which there would be no Christianity on earth today.
4. It is a ministry of the Catholic Church by which Christ continues His own priestly work of saving and sanctifying the souls for whom He shed His blood on Calvary.

We have seen (1) that it is a sacrament of the new law instituted by Christ at the Last Supper and (3) that it is an institution without which there would be no Christianity on earth today.

We can easily understand (4) that it is a ministry of the Catholic Church by which Christ continues His own priestly work of saving and sanctifying the souls for whom He shed His blood on Calvary. Without the priesthood, how could we have Christ's continuing presence among us in the Eucharist to sustain and accompany us? And further, how sad a story would it be, the story of our lives, if it didn't feature the opportunity for frequent Confession, wherein our sins are forgiven with the very power of Christ that He has shared with the priest at ordination? And then there is that other healing sacrament of forgiveness that is no less important for our lasting happiness—the Anointing of the Sick.

It used to be a common custom for Catholics to carry cards in their wallets or wear medals inscribed on the back: "I am a Catholic. In case of emergency, please call a priest." You can still find in Catholic religious stores a four-way medal shaped like a cross with that old familiar wording on the back. But why are priests summoned to the side of the dying? Why have Catholics always been concerned that they have a "holy death," traditionally praying to St. Joseph (who died in the arms of Jesus and Mary) in hope and confidence that a priest will be with them when they leave this earthly life? As we mentioned in an earlier chapter, the power of the Sacrament of the Anointing of the Sick is nothing less than tremendous. At the hour of death, the priest comes with the blessed healing oil, and in this sacrament sin is entirely wiped away, along with the punishment due it. The dying person may be unconscious, or even apparently dead when the sacrament is administered! The Church takes into account that after apparent death the soul may often remain for some time in the body, and medical science and experience alike show evidence to this effect. Similarly, if a person is unconscious when receiving this anointing, the effects prevail—forgiveness of sins and the temporal punishment due them—as long as the person has some fear of God.

Left for us to consider, then, is the second characteristic of the priesthood mentioned by Fr. Hardon: "It is a state of life to which some men are called by a special vocation from God." This particular aspect of the priesthood Fr. Hardon has taken straight from the Council of Trent. That Council clarified Church teaching about the priesthood in response to the confusion of the Protestants who had left the Church to start their own churches. And among the truths taught by Trent was this: When the bishop says at a priestly ordination, "Receive the Holy Spirit," the Holy Spirit is given in a new way to the man ordained a priest, who from that moment on has the indelible mark of the eternal priesthood on his soul.

For this reason, a priest is a priest forever. He will be a priest into eternity, like Christ, in whose priesthood he shares. And if, as sometimes happens, a priest decides for any reason to request laicization and it is granted through the proper channels, this does not mean that he is no longer a priest but rather that he is given permission to refrain from exercising his priestly ministry. As a laicized priest, he is even allowed to marry, but again, this does not take the mark of the priesthood from his soul.

This is an awesome fact, the eternal mark of the priesthood. And it naturally brings up the question, What attitude should we take toward priests? In a time like ours when we are reminded not simply of the human frailty of priests but even of the terrible sins some have committed, what are we to say? We might start with the thought of Jane Austen, who, though not Catholic herself, wrote so admirably, "As I am myself partial to the roman catholic religion, it is with infinite regret that I am obliged to blame the Behaviour of any Member of it."[1] How much more should we who are Catholic regret that we might ever need to speak ill of not merely any other Catholic but those who serve us in Christ's place?

Although initially it seems a strange consolation, every Catholic should know that priests have always been subject to weakness, failure, and sin—because the priesthood, while giving them the power to continue Christ's healing work, does not take away their free will or make them divine. Remember Judas Iscariot?

Jesus Himself tells St. Catherine of Siena in the fourteenth century, in their *Dialogue*, what our attitude to the priesthood should be, and why. He says, plainly, "The sins of the clergy should not lessen your reverence for them," and He goes on to explain:

> The reverence you pay to priests is not actually paid to them but to me, in virtue of the blood I have entrusted to their ministry. If this were not so, you should pay them as much reverence as to anyone else, and no more. It is this ministry of theirs that dictates that you should reverence them and come to them, not for what they are in themselves but for the power I have entrusted to them, if you would receive the sacraments of the Church....

---

1   Jane Austen, *The History of England*, in *The Oxford Illustrated Jane Austen*, ed. R. W. Chapman, vol. 6 (Oxford: Oxford University Press, 1988), 147.

So the reverence belongs not to the ministers, but to me and to this glorious blood made one thing with me because of the union of divinity with humanity. And just as the reverence is done to me, so also is the irreverence, for I have already told you that you must not reverence them for themselves, but for the authority I have entrusted to them. (116)

When we think of the power the priest has by sharing in Christ's own priesthood—the power to bring Christ down upon the altar and feed us His true Body and Blood and the power to forgive our sins and cleanse our souls in the Sacraments of Confession and Anointing of the Sick—we can understand Our Lord's words better. He has allowed each priest to become one with Him, and we can never rightly appreciate or honor the union of every priest with Christ. Sadly, this does not guarantee the priest's personal holiness, and that is why we must pray for priests, daily, whether we are grateful for their ministry to us or faced with their imperfections.

For the record, and I think this is true for most Catholics, the number of holy priests I know—faithful, hardworking, devoted, and devout—far exceeds all those reprehensible priests I have heard about. And how often do we think to pray for priests, in gratitude and petition? When we pray more, God will hear us and pour out the grace we beg of Him to sanctify His (and our) priests.

In their own vocations and quest for sanctity, while there is only one priesthood (Christ's) and one main purpose for it (the Holy Sacrifice of the Mass and the forgiveness of sins), there are different states of life a man may choose within the priesthood. And yes, only men may become priests because as much as Christ honored women, He Himself is a man and so those who become one with Him in the priesthood must be men too.

But when a man discerns a call to the priesthood, how exactly will he follow Christ? He can either promise obedience to the bishop of a specific diocese and so become a diocesan priest, or he can vow obedience to the superior of a religious order, in which case he becomes a religious.

The diocesan priest does not take vows but makes three promises to the Church in the hands of the bishop: first, to say the Divine Office daily; second, to obey the bishop; and third, to live a celibate life in order to remain entirely free to give himself to Christ and His Bride, the Church. The diocesan priest then lives in the particular geographic region of the diocese to which he has promised himself and does not live in community, though he may live in a rectory with other priests assigned to his parish.

The priest entering religious life makes three solemn vows before ordination: first, the vow of poverty; second, the vow of obedience to his religious superior; and third, the vow of chastity, which means a celibate life. While the order may send him to faraway lands or assign him any number of duties, usually the religious priest resides in community, living and praying with other priests of his order.

Each particular religious order has a unique charism (gift of the Holy Spirit) given through its founder, as well as a unique mission in the Church. Often the older religious orders, whatever their full official names, are nicknamed after their sainted founders: thus we have the Benedictines founded by St. Benedict, the Franciscans founded by St. Francis, the Dominicans founded by St. Dominic, and the Carmelites under the patronage of Our Lady of Mt. Carmel. Each order's charism reflects and calls members to imitate a particular perfection of Christ, such as the Benedictines imitating Christ's liturgical prayer; the Franciscans, Christ's poverty; the Dominicans, Christ's teaching and preaching; and the Carmelites, Christ's prayer in solitude.

Each of the religious orders we have mentioned were founded by men who became great saints, and their holiness attracted followers during their lifetimes. The founders, finding themselves surrounded by others seeking to follow the same Gospel way of life, appealed to Rome for permission and approval to live together as a congregation in the Church.

These groups of men would be the "first order" of the religious congregation, but women, too, would want to follow this Gospel way. Hence St. Clare became a disciple of St. Francis in the Franciscan way of following Christ, and then a group of women gathered around her. Thus a second order was founded, one of contemplative religious women: the Poor Clares. Eventually lay people, married or living in the world without taking vows, wanted to follow St. Francis's imitation of Christ, and thus sprung up the third-order Franciscans.

The priests, brothers, and consecrated sisters of an order take vows. (Sisters are called nuns if they are cloistered, remaining within their monasteries, dedicated to a life of prayer.) The third-order members usually make promises more fitting to their lay state, though still with the intention of more closely following the evangelical counsels of poverty, chastity (according to their state in life), and obedience.

Perhaps as your awareness of Christ's love grows, you will hear His invitation to follow Him in the priesthood, in the religious life, or in a third order. But even as you wait to hear His voice, you can obey His invitation by praying for priests: for vocations to the priesthood and for those already ordained. You can pray for religious, that those consecrated already will be faithful to their vocations, and that more will heed Christ's call. And you can pray for missionaries, as Christ requested— those already serving, and that the Master of the harvest will send more—so that the Gospel may continue to spread to the ends of the earth.

Chapter 17

Different Catholic Rites

God knows our whole being. Those who ask for His grace with confidence will not be disappointed. Ask Him to give you all you need.

—St. Charbel, Maronite

As we saw at the outset of this book, the Japanese, who miraculously preserved the Faith through centuries without a priest, did it by hanging on to a few fundamentals. One of these was communion with the pontiff in Rome, even through a long period of complete lack of contact with him.

While communion with the Holy Father is and always has been a prerequisite for remaining in the Church, there are today, and have been from very early on, many different rites within the one, holy, catholic, and apostolic Church. These rites are, according to the *Glossary of the Catechism of the Catholic Church*, "diverse liturgical traditions in which the one catholic and apostolic faith has come to be expressed and celebrated in various cultures and lands." As the *Code of Canons of the Eastern Churches* defines it, "Rite is the liturgical, theological, spiritual and disciplinary heritage, distinguished according to peoples' culture and historical circumstances, that find expression in each autonomous church's way of living the faith."

Did we say "Churches"?

Yes, I'm afraid we did. For while in chapter 1 we distinguished between "Church" and "church" and "churches" (the first being the one, holy, catholic apostolic church, the second and third being church buildings or other religions), it is now time to mention another meaning of "Churches" with a capital *C*.

Within the Holy Catholic Church, there are groups of particular churches that share the heritage of their own rite, law, governance, and traditions (with a small *t*); together these churches form *sui iuris* Churches. *Sui iuris* literally means "of their own laws," or to put it more loosely, "self-governed." These Churches are still under the ultimate authority of the Supreme Pontiff in Rome. Again, the 1990 *Code of Canons of the Eastern Churches* comes to our aid: "A group of Christ's faithful hierarchically linked in accordance with law and given express or tacit recognition by the supreme authority of the Church is in this Code called an autonomous Church."

To get down to brass tacks, there are twenty-four of these autonomous Churches within the Catholic Church. Only one is considered Western—the Latin or Roman Catholic Church; the other twenty-three are Eastern, although churches belonging to these Eastern Churches can be found throughout the West, particularly where members have immigrated.

Why such tremendous diversity within the one barque of Peter? There are at least two clear and beautiful reasons. First, considering this diversity from a divine perspective, "The mystery of Christ is so unfathomably rich that it cannot be exhausted by its expression in any single liturgical tradition" (*CCC*, 1201). And second, from a more human perspective, the many lands into which the Gospel was brought and proclaimed naturally incorporated the mystery of Christ in ways particular to each of their cultures.

When Christ instructed the Apostles (His first bishops) to make disciples of all the nations, they carried all He had taught and commanded them, via the highways and byways, to the major cultural centers of their day: Rome, Antioch, Alexandria. These three cities became the heads of the three major groupings of particular Churches and rites within the one Church founded by Christ, these groupings being the Latin, Antiochian/Syriac, and Alexandrian. We must add, too, Armenian, for it was to Armenia that the Apostles Bartholomew and Thaddeus went, and in AD 301 it became the first country to establish Christianity as the state religion. A few years later in 330, when Emperor Constantine established his capital at Constantinople (previously Byzantium), this city, too, became a religious center. With the help of Sts. Basil and John Chrysostom, Constantinople developed its own liturgical rite from the Liturgy of St. James. This final head of subrites we call Byzantine, and here another distinction becomes necessary.

In 1049 there was a great schism in the Church when the patriarch of Constantinople refused to submit to the authority of the pope. From that time, the Eastern Churches became the Eastern Orthodox Church; and that split, to the present day, causes not only spiritual but also semantic difficulties.

To begin with, the term "orthodox" is often used to refer to someone who conforms to established doctrine. In this vein, we might say someone is an "orthodox Christian" as shorthand for expressing his commitment to the essential tenets of Christianity, such as Jesus' divinity, His Resurrection from the dead, His participation in the inner life of the Blessed Trinity of which He is the Second Person, and so on. Note, however, our small *o* in "orthodox" in this context. When we speak of an Orthodox Christian, with a capital *O*, we refer to a member of the Eastern Orthodox Church.

To further complicate the matter, if we speak of someone as an orthodox Catholic, we usually mean this person closely adheres to the teaching of the Church, which includes obedience to the pope. This is precisely what is missing in members of the Orthodox Churches. The members are usually divided according to national lines and only vaguely united under the titular head-ship of the patriarch of Constantinople, but they agree in their rejection of the pope as head of the one true Church.

Our next semantic difficulty comes with the word "Byzan-tine." Thankfully, some of the Eastern Churches that broke off in the Great Schism have returned to the fold and are now Catholic again, but sadly, there has not been a com-plete reunion of all the churches. Thus there is such a thing as a Byzantine Catholic (one who is under the pope, while belonging to an autonomous Church with the Byzantine rit-ual of the liturgy), and yet this is far removed (as far as East from West) from a Byzantine Orthodox, who is not under the pope but is an Eastern Orthodox Christian.

With these clarifications in mind, then, let's return to our survey of the rites of the Catholic Church and the *sui iuris* Churches contained within them. We list them below with some of their historical and liturgical facts, but keep in mind that many of these Churches are made up of Catholics who, in returning to Rome, were a minority of their Eastern Orthodox counterparts, who still remain separated from Rome in the Eastern Orthodox Churches. That said, here is our list:

Latin Rite

1. **Latin** (or **Roman**) Catholic Church

Alexandrian Rite

Liturgy derived from St. Mark the Evangelist

1. **Coptic** Catholic Church: Egyptian Catholics reunited to Rome in 1741; patriarch of Alexandria; liturgy in Coptic (Egyptian) and Arabic
2. **Eritrean** Catholic Church: descended from Ethiopian Catholic Church but as of 2015 it is its own *sui iuris* Church due to Eritrea's political break from Ethiopia

3. **Ethiopian** Catholic Church: returned to Rome in 1846; liturgy in Geez

West Syrian (or Antiochene) Rite

Liturgy partially in Aramaic, derived from St. James, Apostle

1. **Maronite** Catholic Church: never separated from Rome; country of origin is Lebanon
2. **Syriac** Catholic Church: returned to Rome in 1781 from monophysite heresy; Syriac patriarch of Antioch
3. **Syro-Malankara** Catholic Church: reunited with Rome in 1930; Catholics of Southern India evangelized by St. Thomas, Apostle

Armenian Rite

Liturgy in classical Armenian

1. **Armenian** Catholic Church: returned to Rome at the time of the Crusades

East Syrian (or Chaldean) Rite

Liturgy partially in Aramaic

1. **Chaldean** Catholic Church: Babylonian Catholics returned to Rome in 1692 from Nestorian heresy
2. **Syro-Malabar** Catholic Church: reunited with Rome in sixteenth century from Nestorian heresy; Catholics of Southern India evangelized by St. Thomas, Apostle

Byzantine (or Constantinopolitan) Rite

Two main divine liturgies, first from St. Basil the Great, modification (more commonly used) by St. John Chrysostom

1. **Albanian** Catholic Church: returned to Rome in 1628; liturgical language is Albanian

2. **Belarusian** Catholic Church: returned to Rome in seventeenth century; liturgy in Old Slavonic

3. **Bulgarian** Greek Catholic Church: returned to Rome in 1861; liturgy in Old Slavonic

4. Byzantine Church of Croatia, Serbia, and Montenegro (or **Križevci** Catholic Church): returned to Rome in 1611; Old Slavonic; most Croatians are Roman rite Catholics

5. **Greek Byzantine** Catholic Church: returned to Rome in 1829; liturgy in Greek

6. **Hungarian** Greek Catholic Church: descendants of Ruthenians who returned to Rome in 1646; liturgy in Greek, Hungarian, and English

7. **Italo-Albanian** Catholic Church: never separated from Rome; liturgy in Greek and Italo-Albanian

8. **Macedonian** Catholic Church: established in 2001; descended from Bulgarian and Križevci Catholic Churches

9. **Melkite** Greek Catholic Church: definitive union with Rome in eighteenth century; Melkite Greek patriarch of Damascus; liturgy in Greek, Arabic, English, Portuguese, and Spanish

10. **Romanian** Catholic Church: returned to Rome in 1697; liturgy in Romanian

11. **Russian** Catholic Church: returned to Rome in 1905; liturgy in Old Slavonic

12. **Ruthenian** Catholic Church (also known as the Byzantine Catholic Church in America): returned to Rome in 1596 and 1646; originally from Russia, Hungary, and Croatia

13. **Slovak** Catholic Church

14. **Ukrainian** Greek Catholic Church: reunited with Rome in 1595; patriarch or metropolitan of Lviv; liturgy in Old Slavonic and the vernacular

* * *

What can we say about this vast panoply of Catholic Churches and rites?

Most importantly, we must say that since the seven sacraments were instituted by Christ and require particular matter and form to be valid, there is a commonality of these sacraments in the different rites, and only their accidental features differ (though due to the various languages, cultures, and liturgical customs, these differences in accidents can be quite striking).

So, too, we must acknowledge that there is a difference of authority within the various rites, but as we have seen, this authority (whether of a patriarch or a major archbishop within an autonomous Church) is always under the ultimate authority of the vicar of the universal Church, the pope. For the Eastern Rites, the Supreme Pontiff exercises his authority through the Congregation for the Eastern Churches.

Next, there are different canon laws for the different rites, but these break into two codes only: for the West, the *Code of Canon Law* (1983), and for all the Eastern Rites, the *Code of Canons of the Eastern Churches* (1990).

Finally, one cannot help but appreciate the very richness of the Church. Her absolute maternity allows her to stay so close to the local peoples, so concerned for their contributions to the beauty that she presents to Christ, her all-loving Spouse.

While it is true that those of us in the Latin or Roman Catholic Church belong to the largest autonomous Church among the Catholic Churches, what a gift it is to begin to appreciate the Eastern Rites and Churches. As Pope St. John Paul II said in his 1995 apostolic letter *Orientale Lumen*,

> Our Eastern Catholic brothers and sisters are very conscious of being the living bearers of this tradition, together with our Orthodox brothers and sisters. The members of the Catholic Church of the Latin tradition must also be fully acquainted

with this treasure and thus feel, with the Pope, a passionate longing that the full manifestation of the Church's catholicity be restored to the Church and to the world, expressed not by a single tradition, and still less by one community in opposition to the other; and that we too may be granted a full taste of the divinely revealed and undivided heritage of the universal Church which is preserved and grows in the life of the Churches of the East as in those of the West. (1–2)

And yet even within our Latin family of rites, surprises and a wider tradition than we expect await our attention.

According to Pope Benedict XVI's apostolic letter *Summorum Pontificum* (July 7, 2007), the Roman rite, though still one rite, now has within it both the Ordinary Form and the Extraordinary Form. These are not separate rites, but they offer an amazing breadth of custom. In the Ordinary Form, Mass is celebrated according to the *Missale Romanum* of 1970, the *Novus Ordo Missae*, in its most current edition, and the rituals of the other sacraments are taken from the Latin *typical editions* revised after Vatican Council II. In the Extraordinary Form, Mass is celebrated according to the *Missale Romanum* of 1962, and the other sacraments according to the *Roman Ritual* in use at the time of Vatican Council II.

There is sometimes confusion between the Roman and Latin rite, but the family of Latin rites is more extensive. It includes the Roman rite, but in addition the Mozarabic rite (from the sixth century at least, along the Iberian peninsula), the Ambrosian rite (from Milan, consolidated by St. Ambrose), the Bragan rite (from Portugal, twelfth century or earlier), and the "order rites" such as the Dominican, Carmelite, and Carthusian rites (dating from the thirteenth, twelfth, and eleventh centuries, respectively).

As to the twenty-three Eastern Catholic Churches, we can only add to our brief notes above that if you have the opportunity to participate in their liturgies or learn more of their customs, take advantage of such graces, and let this brief introduction be an open door rather than a shaded window.

Chapter 18

The Bible and Tradition

Ignorance of the Scriptures is ignorance of Christ.

— St. Jerome

Perhaps the silliest myth on the planet is the one that claims that Catholics do not know or love the Bible, that the Bible has been the book of the Protestants, and that Catholics have been somehow prevented from knowing and loving it.

We can see from our epigraph at the head of this chapter that St. Jerome insisted on knowledge of the Bible as a prerequisite for knowing Christ, our Savior. It would be hard to find a greater authority on the Bible than St. Jerome, one of the four great Latin Fathers of the Church, unless we consider the other three Latin Fathers (also, all four, Doctors of the Church): his contemporary St. Augustine; Augustine's mentor, St. Ambrose; and the pope of a century later, St. Gregory the Great.

St. Augustine, for his part, exhorted the faithful, "Let us therefore yield ourselves and bow to the authority of the Holy Scriptures, which can neither err nor deceive." He said of the Bible, "Letters have reached us too from that city, apart from which we are wandering: those letters are the Scriptures."[1] His

---

1   St. Augustine, *Expositions on the Psalms, in Nicene and Post-Nicene Fathers*, vol. 8, ed. Philip Schaff, D.D., LL.D. (Massachusetts: Hendrickson Publishers), 450.

On Christian Doctrine is a spectacular introduction and guide to reading and interpreting Scripture, and his other writings are bursting with quotes from the Bible and his profound interpretations of everything from Genesis to Revelation.

St. Ambrose, who baptized Augustine, said in a letter to Constantius, a new bishop,

> The Divine Scripture is a sea, containing in it deep meanings, and an abyss of prophetic mysteries; and into this sea enter many rivers. There are sweet and transparent streams, cool fountains too there are, springing up into life eternal, and pleasant words as a honey-comb. Agreeable sentences too there are, refreshing the minds of the hearers, if I may say so, with spiritual drink, and soothing them with the sweetness of their moral precepts.[2]

Another of their contemporaries, and another Father of the Church, St. John Chrysostom, had this to say in his homily on John 4:20, "The Holy Scriptures were not given us for this only, that we might have them in books, but that we might engrave them on our hearts."[3]

And what about that fourth great Latin Father, Pope St. Gregory the Great? We have the words of another great pontiff, Pope Benedict XVI, when he "returned to the extraordinary figure of Pope Gregory the Great to receive some additional light from his rich teaching." Pope Benedict noted that "he left us numerous works, from which the Church in successive centuries has drawn with both hands."[4] Such is the Church's attitude toward all the Fathers and Doctors; she is ever ready to plunder their treasures, since their riches are

---

2   St. Ambrose, *The Letters of S. Ambrose, Bishop of Milan* (Oxford: James Parker, 1881), 6.
3   St. John Chrysostom, *Homilies on the Gospel of St. John*, in *Nicene and Post-Nicene Fathers*, ed. Philip Schaff, D.D., LL.D., vol. 14 (Massachusetts: Hendrickson Publishers), 114.
4   Pope Benedict XVI, *Church Fathers and Teachers: From Saint Leo to Peter Lombard* (San Francisco: Ignatius Press, 2010), 43.

none other than those of Christ Himself, which He rejoices to share with all His children. The Fathers of the Church are inspired by the Holy Spirit to a degree just short of the scriptural authors, and the earliest of them knew the Apostles. The Doctors of the Church (some of them also Fathers) span the centuries into modern times. There are thirty-six, all of whom the popes have named for their eminent doctrine; you can find a list of these singular teachers in the last chapter of this book.

Regarding Pope St. Gregory, Pope Benedict continued, "He was a passionate reader of the Bible, which he approached not simply with a speculative purpose: from Sacred Scripture, he thought, the Christian must draw not theoretical understanding so much as the daily nourishment for his soul."[5] Clearly our myth of Catholic dismissal of the Bible is busted. But how and when did it arise?

This myth is not new. Hilaire Belloc in his book *Survivals and New Arrivals* addresses the biblical attack on the Church: "that is, the comparison of Catholic doctrine, morals, and practice, to their disadvantage, with the words of Holy Writ, regarded as a final authority in the Literal meaning of every word there found."[6] Belloc identifies this attitude as what we in the States call Fundamentalism, whereas he notes it is called, "on our side of the Atlantic, 'the attitude of the Bible Christian.'"[7]

Belloc was naming an old attack that originated with one whom we might call the founder of Protestantism, the confused and disillusioned Catholic priest Martin Luther. In 1520, Luther claimed it was Catholic teaching (to which he vehemently objected) that only the pope can authentically interpret Scripture. As with many of his statements, he was

---

5   Ibid., 44.
6   Hilaire Belloc, *Survivals and New Arrivals* (London: Sheed and Ward, 1929), 52–53.
7   Ibid., 53.

mistaken. Luther was neither the first nor the last to reject what he thought was the Church, when in fact he erred. As Archbishop Fulton Sheen said in more recent times, "There are not one hundred people in the United States who hate the Catholic Church, but there are millions who hate what they wrongly perceive the Catholic Church to be."[8]

Another myth that takes us back to Luther is the one that praises him as the first to translate the Bible into the vernacular. In fact, the very first Bible we know of in German dates from the eighth century, produced by the monastery of Monse. By Luther's own time, there were thirty-six thousand German manuscript Bibles in the land, and five years before his German translation, a complete copy of the Bible in German had been printed. But this argument about the Church's keeping the Bible from the common people takes us back—in our vindication of the truth—even further, again to St. Jerome.

The Old Testament books had been written in Hebrew, but because the dominant language of the Roman Empire was Greek, the early Church used a Greek translation called the Septuagint (from the Latin *septuaginta*, meaning "seventy," which was the number of translators said to have produced it). The New Testament books had been written in Greek, so all the books of the Bible were available in the language of the people, but in the fourth century, Latin began to replace Greek in the Western part of the Roman Empire.

Precisely because Holy Mother Church was concerned that the Bible remain accessible to her children, in the year 384, Pope Damasus asked his secretary Jerome—a faithful and extremely educated priest with a gift for languages—to compose an official Latin text of the Bible. Jerome was so obedient

---

8   Fulton J. Sheen, *The Cries of Jesus from the Cross: A Fulton Sheen Anthology* (Manchester, New Hampshire: Sophia Institute Press, 2018), xi.

to his commission and had such a great love for Christ and Scripture that he ended up in Palestine for thirty-five years, continually working at his task. He completed his work about the year 405 and spent the remainder of his life writing extensive commentaries on the biblical books.

In the thirteenth century, St. Jerome's Latin translation of the Bible became known as the Vulgate because it was the *vulgata editio*, the edition in general circulation—or, in other words, the edition prepared for the crowd, the *vulgus*, the common people.

But here we run into another popular misconception about the Bible. Having traced its translations, we need to ask about the original. Where did *it* come from? I admit I have often vaguely thought it must have come, like the Ten Commandments, all of a piece from heaven—or in two pieces, like the two tablets: the Old Testament and New Testament written on two different scrolls. The reality is much less simple, but for simplicity's sake, here is the short version.

During the time of Christ, there were several lists of the books of the Old Testament Scriptures proposed by different Jewish groups, but no one agreed upon one authoritative list of the Hebrew canon—those books inspired by the Holy Spirit and worthy to be considered sacred in the strongest sense. After Christ's Ascension, His disciples not only spread His message in their missions and preaching but also eventually began to write the Gospel of His life, Death, and Resurrection. The Catholic Church, over time, discerned what was and was not inspired among these writings—that is, of both the Old and New Testaments. The Councils of Hippo (AD 393) and Carthage (AD 397 and 419) determined the canon of Scripture as we have it today.

About a thousand years later, the Council of Florence affirmed the canon. But not too long afterward, Martin Luther rejected the seven Deuterocanonical ("second canon")

Books. These seven books of the Old Testament were, in Luther's time, available only in Greek, and he rejected them, considering them as part of a second and nonauthoritative, uninspired Greek canon. Since then manuscripts have surfaced that affirm the Hebrew and Aramaic origin of these books, but the Church had already, with the help of the Holy Spirit, discerned long before that these books—called by the Protestants "the apocrypha"—are indeed truly part of Holy Scripture.

Finally, in the mid-1500s, the Council of Trent convened to correct the errors of the Protestant revolt. One of Trent's gifts was to dogmatically name the books in the canon of Scripture. The books and the canon did not change, but the Council Fathers officially defined them so the faithful would have absolute clarity. The Vulgate was then named the official and authentic edition of the Bible.

What about Luther's contention that the Church allowed only the pope to interpret the Scriptures? The Council of Trent, in this same fourth session held on April 8, 1546, explained that the Church's concern was not with maintaining a singular authority of the pope in biblical matters but rather with safeguarding the whole Tradition of the Church. And so Trent decreed,

> Furthermore, in order to restrain petulant spirits, It decrees that no one, relying on his own skill shall—in matters of faith, and of morals pertaining to the edification of Christian doctrine— wresting the sacred Scripture to his own senses, presume to interpret the said sacred Scripture contrary to that sense which holy mother Church—whose it is to judge of the true sense and interpretation of the holy Scriptures—hath held and doth hold; or even contrary to the unanimous consent of the Fathers; even though such interpretations were never (intended) to be at any time published.

The Council then went on to impose a restraint on the printing of Bibles—but it was not the restraint one might suppose, given the charges made against the Church about her keeping the Bible from her children. Far from such a prohibitive attitude, the Church wanted simply to protect the faithful from the falsely proposed commentaries, interpretations, and biblical texts that the Protestants had been circulating. The Council required that printers would from that point on print the books of Scripture with the license of ecclesiastical superiors so that the notes and comments included would be approved, not be published anonymously or under false names, and further that the Vulgate would "be printed in the most correct manner possible."

The decrees of the Council of Trent were careful to safeguard not only Holy Scripture itself but also the connection between its interpretation and Tradition. We do not have to rely solely on the Council of Trent, though, for our understanding of the Church's teaching on Scripture, for we have another more recent Council to help us.

In the opening paragraph of *Dei Verbum*, the Second Vatican Council's dogmatic constitution on Divine Revelation, we read, "Therefore, following in the footsteps of the Council of Trent and of the First Vatican Council, this present council wishes to set forth authentic doctrine on divine revelation and how it is handed on, so that by hearing the message of salvation, the whole world may believe, and by believing it may hope, and by hoping it may love" (1). This authentic doctrine on Divine Revelation that Vatican II sets forth can be explained as follows: After Christ, having given authority to Peter to guard His flock, ascended into heaven, the Holy Spirit descended on the first bishops, the Apostles. These Apostles and the other disciples of the Lord spread His teaching, going forth to baptize the nations. "[Christ's] commission was fulfilled, too, by those Apostles and apostolic men who under the inspiration of the same Holy Spirit committed the message of salvation to writing. But in order to keep the Gospel forever whole and alive within the Church, the Apostles left bishops as their successors, 'handing over' to them 'the authority to teach in their own place' " (7). This means that "Sacred tradition and Sacred Scripture form one sacred deposit of the word of God, committed to the Church" (10).

But what about interpreting this double gift of revelation, our Sacred Tradition and Scripture? We can see from the Protestant experience that allowing each person to interpret Scripture on his own leads to the splintering of one church into thousands. If we with so little vision can see this, how much more did God foresee it? And so this task of authentic interpretation of revelation "has been entrusted exclusively to the living teaching office of the Church" (*Dei Verbum*, 10).

The consequence is what we might call a three-legged stool. Without any one of the legs, the stool will fall, while with all three, it stays upright: "It is clear, therefore, that sacred tradition, Sacred Scripture and the teaching authority of the Church, in accord with God's most wise design, are so linked and joined together that one cannot stand without the others, and that all together and each in its own way under the action of the one Holy Spirit contribute effectively to the salvation of souls" (*Dei Verbum*, 10).

As to the acquaintance of any particular Catholic with Holy Scripture, that is another question. As we mentioned in an earlier chapter, the Church reads the Bible as liturgy. Thus the more a Catholic takes advantage of the rich daily liturgy of the Church—both the Mass (or Divine Liturgy, for Eastern Catholics) and the Liturgy of the Hours—the more he will come to know the Bible.

In addition, as we heard from the Church Fathers at the beginning of this chapter, the faithful have always been encouraged to read and meditate on the Bible in their personal prayer. If we jump forward a few centuries, we find Pope St. Pius X confessing in his pontificate about a hundred years ago, "Nothing would please us more than to see our beloved children form the habit of reading the Gospels—not merely from time to time, but every day."

We started with St. Jerome as our biblical teacher, and we cannot do better than take his advice to Eustochius as a model for our own relationship with Holy Scripture: "Read assiduously and learn as much as you can. Let sleep find you holding your Bible, and when your head nods let it be resting on the sacred page."

Chapter 19

How to Pray

Prayer is the place of refuge for every worry, a foundation for cheerfulness, a source of constant happiness, a protection against sadness.

—St. John Chrysostom

As St. John Chrysostom hints above, prayer is no place for worry. It is rather—and he states this plainly—a refuge from it. And yet we can find ourselves confused and anxious about how to pray, afraid that our prayer is too little, too late, or displeasing to God because of our distractions (those pesky thoughts that swarm around us like gnats) or our ignorance of what to say that might be pleasing to Him.

Accordingly, there are a few preliminaries we must address without delay. The truth is that God is our loving Father, and He delights in attending to our prayer even as He knows, and has known from all eternity, that we have no idea what we are doing. He made us, and so He knows perfectly of what we are made.

St. Thomas Aquinas, that man of a million insights, explained, "The human mind is unable to remain aloft for long on account of the weakness of nature, because human weakness weighs down the soul to the level of inferior things: and hence it is that when, while praying, the mind ascends to

157

God by contemplation, of a sudden it wanders off through weakness" (*Summa Theologiae*, IIa-IIae, q. 83, a. 13). Whether you are used to ascending to God in contemplation or merely trying to make it through your morning prayer with some attention, you have no doubt felt this weakness of nature and the intrusion of inferior things (thinking of what your breakfast will be, for instance). The good news is that God knows our weakness and loves us nonetheless.

The key, though, to continually opening the door of His Heart is not worrying about this weakness. Happily, as St. Thomas also explains in the same place, "It is not necessary that prayer should be attentive throughout, because the force of the original intention with which one sets about praying renders the whole prayer meritorious." In other words, by intending to pray and beginning with a desire to lift your mind and heart to God, you have already won your Father's attention and His mercy. What remains is to do your poor best to stay in His presence until your prayer time is finished. That time might be only a moment, as when you pass a Catholic church and acknowledge the Blessed Sacrament there with the Sign of the Cross; or it might be a half hour spent with Him in a place of silence and solitude, such as your bedroom; or for busy mothers of young families, it might be a needed retreat of five minutes sitting on the floor in the bathroom with the door locked to keep out the little Christians.

When we consider the types of prayer you might engage in, there are several divisions we could make. There is the division between vocal prayer—prayer out loud—and mental prayer, which is silent prayer. There is the division between liturgical prayer and private prayer, as well as the division between communal prayer and prayer alone. There is the division of prayer according to its ends: intercession, to obtain something from God; repentance, to ask His forgiveness; praise, to glorify His greatness; gratitude, to thank

Him. There is even a division according to methods—such as Ignatian prayer, which begins with a meditation on a scene in the life of Christ and progresses to a conversation with Him, and *lectio divina*, in which we read Scripture slowly, letting the Word of God resonate deep within us. But finally, overarching all these divisions and covering every type, prayer is simply communication with God.

When the disciples lived with Jesus, they observed Him praying frequently. He prayed in public and in private, in the synagogue and outdoors, in the day and at night, aloud and silently. They asked Him, finally, to teach them to pray, and He gave the words of the Our Father. In this prayer is contained everything we need to speak to God, and so the saints tell us stories of how perfect union with God can come from praying it well.

The Church's Doctor of Prayer, St. Teresa of Jesus of Avila, tells the story of a Carmelite nun who thought she could not pray because she never made it through a single Our Father. She was held back by the opening words, reflecting until her prayer time was up on the wonder of addressing God as "Our Father" and all the love and truth this first phrase contained. This nun, whom St. Teresa holds up as an exemplar for our prayer, was considering who God was and who she was.

Since God is our all-loving Father and Creator and we are His beloved children, this is a reflection worth pondering, and it leads to what Teresa's contemporary St. Ignatius recommends when he encourages us to approach God "by speaking exactly as one friend speaks to another . . . now asking him for a favor, now blaming himself for some misdeed, now making known his affairs to him, and seeking advice in them."[1] If friendship with God seems irreverent, recall that Jesus

---

1   St. Ignatius of Loyola, *The Spiritual Exercises of St. Ignatius*, ed. John F. Thornton, trans. Louis J. Puhl (New York: Random House, 2000), 24.

Himself told us the night before He died, "No longer do I call you servants, for the servant does not know what his master is doing; but I have called you friends, for all that I have heard from my Father I have made known to you" (John 15:15).

St. Teresa spoke often of friendship with God. Boldly and aptly, when she had fallen off the back of a cart into the mud, she said to Him, "If this is how You treat Your friends, no wonder You have so few!"[2] This is friendship at its most natural, and though she was being funny, Teresa did not take back this repartee because authentic conversation was at the heart of her prayer. As she teaches in the eighth chapter of her autobiography, "Mental prayer in my opinion is nothing else than an intimate sharing between friends; it means taking time frequently to be alone with Him who we know loves us."[3]

Just before giving this definition, St. Teresa invites us, "Whoever has not begun the practice of prayer, I beg for the love of the Lord not to go without so great a good. There is nothing here to fear but only something to desire ... at least a person will come to understand the road leading to heaven." Soon after she repeats, "I don't know what they fear who fear to begin the practice of mental prayer."[4]

What is convincing about the saints is their echo of the Divine Word. Just as Jesus repeatedly told us, "Do not be afraid," and "Do not be anxious," and "Fear not, little flock," so His friends repeat His reassurance. We have just heard the great St. Teresa telling us in the sixteenth century not to be afraid of prayer; closer to our own day we find the little St. Thérèse echoing her holy mother's (and Jesus') words in a letter to the priest who was her spiritual brother. Little Thérèse

---

2   A recounting of this famous incident is found in *The Life of St. Teresa* translated by Alice Lady Lovat "from the French of a Carmelite nun" and published in 1912 by Simpkin, Marshall, Hamilton, Kent and Co. Ltd.

3   St. Teresa of Avila, *The Book of Her Life*, Collected Works, vol. I (Washington, DC: ICS Publications, 1987), 96.

4   Ibid.

writes to Fr. Roulland, "I do not understand souls who fear a Friend so tender," and then goes on to tell him about her own experience of prayer.

Thérèse's prayer, like everything about her, was very simple. As the *Catechism* quotes from her *Story of a Soul* to begin its own section on prayer, "For me, prayer is a surge of the heart; it is a simple look turned toward heaven, it is a cry of recognition and of love, embracing both trial and joy" (quoted in *CCC*, 2558). She gives a fuller explanation in her letter to Fr. Roulland, writing,

> At times, when I am reading certain spiritual treatises in which perfection is shown through a thousand obstacles, surrounded by a crowd of illusions, my poor little mind quickly tires; I close the learned book that is breaking my head and drying up my heart, and I take up Holy Scripture. Then all seems luminous to me; a single word uncovers for my soul infinite horizons, perfection seems simple to me, I see it is sufficient to recognize one's nothingness and to abandon oneself as a child into God's arms. Leaving to great souls, to great minds the beautiful books I cannot understand, much less put into practice, I rejoice at being little since children alone and those who resemble them will be admitted to the heavenly banquet.[5]

Her hints on prayer include, then, reading Scripture, discovering in it those verses that God is directing to us personally, and abandoning ourselves in gratitude and confidence into His loving care. And yet if this way of prayer does not appeal to you, keep in mind the Little Flower's next words: "I am very happy there are many mansions in God's kingdom, for if there were only the one whose description and road

---

5   St. Thérèse of Lisieux, Letter 226, May 9, 1987, in *General Correspondence*, vol. 2, trans. John Clarke, O.C.D. (Washington DC: ICS Publications, 1988), 1093–94.

seems incomprehensible to me, I would not be able to enter there."[6] If you find her description of the mansion and the road to it rather incomprehensible, fear not; there are many other saints ready to teach you how to pray!

St. Isidore of Seville, for instance, another Doctor of the Church, advises in a general way, "Prayer purifies us, reading instructs us. Both are good when both are possible. If we want to be always in God's company, we must pray regularly and read regularly. When we pray, we talk to God, when we read, God talks to us."[7] St. Teresa of Avila, too, recommended always bringing a book to prayer. It's merely a matter of finding a spiritual book that helps you talk to God and listen to Him. Scripture always takes first place, but many other classic and modern books are at our disposal.

We ought to address, however, the particular prayers every Catholic should know—the prayers proposed and recommended by the Church, our teacher and our Mother.

In the first place is the Mass, the prayer and sacrifice of Christ perpetuated in an unbloody manner on the altar. We are required to attend Mass once a week on Sundays precisely because it is the ultimate prayer and the Church cannot risk our missing out. If you are able to attend Mass more frequently, all the better.

Next there is that other great liturgical prayer, the Liturgy of the Hours or Divine Office. Its primary components, like hinges on a door opening into the whole treasury of the Church's psaltery (the Psalms), are morning and evening prayer. These are wonderful "hours" to start with, and you may find they are the perfect beginning and end to your day. They are part of the official prayer of the Church, and by

---

6   Ibid.
7   *The Office of Readings: According to the Roman Rite*, trans. ICEL (Boston: Daughters of St. Paul, 1983), 1379.

participating you join in with countless priests and religious scattered over the globe, helping them sanctify the day for the whole world.

After the Holy Sacrifice of the Mass and the Liturgy of the Hours, the most valuable prayer of the Church is most likely the Rosary. It was given to St. Dominic by Our Lady in the thirteenth century and has been recommended ever since by so many popes and saints, enriched with so many promises and indulgences, and urged so often by Our Lady in her apparitions that we can only trust that it has much more in it than we might initially imagine. The key to the Rosary is joining mental prayer, or consideration of the scriptural mysteries of the Rosary, with the repeated vocal prayers of ten Hail Marys, one Our Father, and one Glory Be for each decade. This combination, along with the passing of the beads through one's fingers, engages the whole of us: our bodies, our minds, our hearts, and our voices. Pope St. John Paul II, as well as St. Padre Pio, called this his favorite prayer. John Paul II added to its traditional three sets of mysteries a fourth so that the entire life of Christ would be material for our meditation. As the oldest little shepherd of Fatima said, "The Most Holy Virgin in these last times in which we live has given a new efficacy to the recitation of the Rosary to such an extent that there is no problem, no matter how difficult it is that we cannot resolve by the prayer of the Rosary."

Worthy of mention after the Rosary is a prayer of more recent vintage that is said, also, on the rosary beads: the Divine Mercy Chaplet. It has been remarkable to witness, over the past forty years, the progressive elevation of the Divine Mercy devotion by the Church, as she discovered its treasures and ratified its authenticity.

In the 1930s, Jesus appeared to a Polish nun named Sister Faustina. To her He revealed, as she wrote in her *Divine Mercy Diary*, that He wanted a picture painted, a chaplet and annual Eastertide novena introduced, and a feast on the second Sunday after Easter. Poor Sister Faustina! These were a lot of directives for a poor, humble, unknown nun. And yet, in God's providence, it all came to be. In the Jubilee Year 2000, Pope St. John Paul II canonized Faustina and instituted the Feast of Divine Mercy on the second Sunday after Easter. With that, the Divine Mercy image, chaplet, and novena (which begins on Good Friday and leads to the Feast of Divine Mercy) received universal recognition.

You will find a short explanation on how to say the Rosary and the Divine Mercy Chaplet in the last chapter of this book.

Having addressed liturgical and vocal prayers, what can we say about mental prayer, which the saints so highly recommend? We conclude with three pieces of advice.

The first is from St. Thérèse, but she got it from St. John of the Cross, the Mystical Doctor. They say, "We can never have too much confidence in the good God; He is so mighty and so merciful. We obtain from Him as much as we hope for."[8] This means we should hope for a great deal! As St. Thérèse also said, to expect little from God is to put a limit on His omnipotence, to practically insult Him. So ask away. Pray, hope, and don't worry, in the words of St. Padre Pio.

The second piece of advice is more a fragment of wisdom that goes like this: "Pray as you can, not as you ought." We must remember, as St. Alphonsus told us, that "our prayers are so dear to God, that He has appointed the angels to present them to Him as soon as they come forth from our mouths."[9] This means we can approach God with the eagerness of small children who want to tell their loving parents everything, and this precludes slavish fear.

---

8   Francois Jamart, O.C.D., *Complete Spiritual Doctrine of St. Thérèse of Lisieux* (New York: Alba House, 2001), 8.

9   St. Alphonsus de Ligouri, *The Great Means of Salvation and of Perfection* (Brooklyn: Redemptorist Fathers, 1927), 50.

Our third bit of advice comes from St. Teresa of Avila, who suggested that we take a comfortable position when we pray, though perhaps not so comfortable that we immediately fall asleep. A comfortable position makes sense because, although kneeling is a time-honored posture for prayer (and fitting, before the Divine Majesty), sitting is the usual posture we take when conversing with a friend. You want to have a long chat with God, telling Him everything. Jesus is your brother, your best friend, your Savior, and your Spouse. He wants to hear as much as you have to say—He is one friend who won't get bored, and His eyes won't glaze over! He loves you and is fascinated by a single glance, as the Song of Songs attests.

St. Thérèse (the little one) did often fall asleep during her prescribed times of prayer. In the chapel she would fall asleep kneeling and later wake to find her head on the floor once again. This understandably bothered her; after all, her primary job as a Carmelite was to pray. But then one day she was inspired to see this awkward situation through the eyes of Love. It occurred to her that parents delight in gazing on their sleeping children, and so God, the ultimate Father, must delight in seeing His children asleep too. St. Thérèse reminds us as she reminded her sister Leonie, "God is even kinder than you think. He is satisfied with a look, a sigh of love."[10] So do not be afraid, little flock. Your Father is pleased to give you the kingdom of heaven, and He only waits for you to ask.

---

10 St. Thérèse of Lisieux, *Collected Letters*, trans. F.J. Sheed (New York: Sheed and Ward, 1949), 275.

Chapter 20

Last Things and Indulgences

I urge you to remain steadfast in faith, so that at last we will all reach heaven and there rejoice together.

—St. Andrew Kim Taegon

Just as there will surely be an end to this book, so there will surely be an end to each of our lives on earth. And just as there are some last things an author and reader want to cover at the close of a book, so the end of our lives will contain a similar wrapping up, which the Church calls the four last things.

The four last things are traditionally named as death, judgment, heaven, and hell. But our hope is that the four last things awaiting the end of our particular journeys will be death, judgment, purgatory, and heaven; or if we are very hopeful, we might reduce our list to three—namely, death, judgment, and heaven.

Before we get carried away, let's consider the original (or rather final) four. Death is coming to us all, whether sooner or later, but we know by faith (and even by reason, as Aristotle shows in *De Anima*, his book on the soul) that the soul is immortal. St. Athanasius puts it this way: "For God would not be true if, after saying that we would die, the human being did not die. On the other hand, it was improper that what had once been made rational and partakers of his Word should perish, and once again return to non-being through corruption."[1] And so, as St. Thérèse expressed it near the end of her short life, "I am not dying, I am entering into Life."[2] She had the confidence of a saint: not confidence in her own goodness but rather confidence in the mercy of God. She wrote at the end of *Story of a Soul*, "Yes, I feel it; even though I had on my conscience all the sins that can be committed, I would go, my heart broken with sorrow, and throw myself into Jesus' arms, for I know how much He loves the prodigal child who returns to Him."[3] St. Thérèse knew she was going to eternal life, and we should share her hope.

But we must, at the same time, acknowledge what awaits those who refuse Jesus' loving embrace, those who will not throw themselves into Jesus' arms. In that case it would not be eternal life but eternal death. In the words of St. Ambrose, "I stand between two eternities. I must fall either into one or the other."[4] Since eternal life is held out to us by God, who sent His only Son to save us, let us be careful to fall in that direction!

I remember when I was in labor with my first son. There was a moment in the hospital when I realized I couldn't get out of it: this baby would be born, one way or another. And so, too, with our birth into eternity. For each of us at death there will be that moment of meeting God, and the particular judgment for each of our souls; there is no way to avoid it. There and then, "at the evening of life, we shall be judged on our love," as St. John of the Cross taught. The *Catechism* explains, "Each man receives his eternal retribution in his immortal soul at the very moment of his death, in a particular judgment that

1   St. Athanasius, *On the Incarnation*, trans. John Behr (Yonkers, New York: St. Vladimir's Seminary Press, 2011), 55.
2   St. Thérèse of Lisieux, Letter 244, June 9, 1897, in *General Correspondence*, vol. II, trans. John Clarke, O.C.D. (Washington DC: ICS Publications, 1988), 1128.
3   St. Thérèse of Lisieux, *Story of a Soul*, trans. John Clarke, O.C.D. (Washington, DC: ICS Publications), 259.
4   *The Catholic Church: The Teacher of Mankind* (New York: Office of Catholic Publications, 1905), 109.

refers his life to Christ: either entrance into the blessedness of heaven—through a purification or immediately—or immediate and everlasting damnation" (1022).

The attitude every Catholic can cultivate is well expressed by St. Camillus de Lellis: "The approach of death is indeed the best news I could hear. A man must once pay the forfeit of death, and I do not value this life at a farthing if only our Lord will give me a tiny corner in paradise."[5] St. Camillus knew that the eternal bliss of heaven will so far eclipse every happiness of this life, not to mention our present sufferings, that the only rational response to what awaits us is joyful hope. If a salutary fear is present also, let that serve to remind us to trust God completely and to live close to the sacraments and graces of the Church, our loving Mother, who has no intention of letting us die unprepared.

Holy Mother Church has much to do, however, before we are prepared. Even for the most saintly among us, those who have never stained their souls with mortal sin, there is still the dross of venial sin to burn off. If this seems harsh on God's part, consider how the saints describe our anticipated first encounter with Him. St. Catherine of Genoa, who received revelations on purgatory—that place of purification between earth and heaven—says, "I see Paradise has no gate, but whosoever will may enter therein, for God is all mercy and stands with open arms to admit us to His glory. But still I see that the Being of God is so pure (far more than one can imagine) that should a soul see in itself even the least mote of imperfection, it would rather cast itself into a thousand hells than go with that spot into the presence of the Divine Majesty."[6]

What is necessary before we can see God face-to-face and want to remain in His all-pure presence is a renewed purity of our souls that have been tainted by sin. Furthermore, our

---

5   Jill Haak Adels, *The Wisdom of the Saints* (New York: Oxford University Press, 1989), 196.
6   St. Catherine of Genoa, *Treatise on Purgatory* (London: Burns & Oates, 1870), 22.

wills, in order to want God completely, must be detached from sin. This renewed purity and righting of the will can be attained in several ways.

The first is by suffering in this life, offered to God in union with Christ's sufferings.

The second is by good works, by which we atone for our temporal punishment (this is the punishment due to God in amends for our sins) and also direct our souls to the good.

The third is by "a conversion which proceeds from a fervent charity," which can "attain the complete purification of the sinner in such a way that no punishment would remain" (*CCC*, 1472, taking this statement from the teaching of the Council of Trent).

The fourth is by indulgences. The best way we can begin to understand this oft-misunderstood gift of the Church is by considering, first, these words of Jesus:

> Which one of you, if his son asks him for bread, will give him a stone? Or if he asks for a fish, will give him a serpent? If you then, who are evil, know how to give good gifts to your children, how much more will your Father who is in heaven give good things to those who ask Him! (Matthew 7:9–11)

Jesus reminds us that even in our selfish imperfection, we do have the goodness to give good things to our children. Not only that, but He reminds us in His other parables of the willingness of those in authority, when pressed, to be merciful, despite their initial resistance. When one is not only just but also merciful—and we do see this even among ourselves "who are evil"—we call that being indulgent. A mother knows her older child does not absolutely need her to do the many kind things she does for him, but she indulges her child because she loves him. Similarly, Holy Mother Church, having been given by Christ the ability to bind and loose and share His riches with her children, cannot resist indulging us because, for Christ's sake, she loves us.

In 1967, Pope St. Paul VI issued an apostolic constitution, *Indulgentiarum Doctrina*, which is one of the most beautiful documents the Church has given to us in modern times. It begins, "The teaching and practice regarding indulgences prevailing for centuries in the Catholic Church rest on divine revelation as their firm foundation."[7] The footnote to this first sentence informs us, from the Council of Trent, that "the power of granting indulgences has been given to the Church by Christ and the Church has used this divinely bestowed power even from its earliest days." Pope Paul goes on to explain the punishment due to sin and the need for genuine conversion of spirit to "restore friendship with God and make expiation for the affront to His wisdom and goodness"(3), as well as the need to repair the injustice or imbalance effected in the moral order by sin. Then he explicates the doctrine of the Communion of Saints, "the life of each of God's children in Christ and through Christ conjoined with the life of all other Christians," whether in heaven, on earth, or in purgatory. Between the members of the Mystical Body, the Communion of Saints, there is "the continuing bond of charity and an abundant exchange of all good things" (5).

These good things are called the Church's treasury, which does not refer to the material goods the Church may have accrued over the centuries.

> On the contrary the "treasury of the Church" is the infinite value, which can never be exhausted, which Christ's merits have before God. They were offered so that the whole of mankind could be set free from sin and attain communion with the Father. (*CCC*, 1476)

---

7 Paul VI, Apostolic Constitution on Indulgences *Indulgentiarum doctrina* (January 1, 1967), in *The Handbook of Indulgences: Norms and Grants* (New York: Catholic Book Publishing: 1991), 99.

> The treasury of the Church is Christ the Redeemer Himself: in Him the atonement and merit of His redemption exist and are at work. Added to this treasure is also the vast, incalculable, ever increasing value in God's eyes of the prayers and good works of the Blessed Virgin Mary and all the saints. (*Indulgentiarum doctrina*, 5)

The Church, then, having both the power (given to her by Christ) to bind and loose and access this treasury of infinite value, can intervene and "indulge" her children by sharing with them this treasury of merits to obtain from the Father the remission of the temporal punishment due to their sins. And yet, being a prudent Mother, she does not give these merits out indiscriminately; rather, she invites her children to particular good works and acts of devotion so they may help her unlock the graces of Christ's merits. Holy Mother Church specifies with precision which works and acts may gain what type of indulgence, and by this she spurs us on to participate in the ancient devotions that have proven most helpful for making saints, even while she indulges us.

Indulgences are of two types: plenary, in which all temporal punishment is wiped away; and partial, in which some temporal punishment is wiped away. Moreover, an indulgence may be gained for oneself or offered for a soul in purgatory (perhaps for a friend or family member who has died or for an unknown inhabitant of that place of purification). As the norms of the apostolic constitution state, "Both partial and plenary indulgences are always applicable to the dead as suffrages."[8] A plenary indulgence can be gained only once a day (except on the day of one's death), while partial indulgences can usually be gained several times a day.

So what must be done to gain an indulgence? Each indulgence is attached to a particular act, and a person in the state

---

8   *Indulgentiarum doctrina*, Norms, N.3.

of grace must do the act to gain the indulgence. For instance, a partial indulgence is granted to the Christian faithful who, in a spirit of penitence, voluntarily abstain from something that is licit for and pleasing to them. So if you offer up the sacrifice of cream in your coffee one morning, that gains a partial indulgence (the remission of some temporal punishment) for you or for someone in purgatory, depending on whether you offer it for yourself or a poor soul.

In the case of plenary indulgences—that is, the remission of *all* temporal punishment due to one's sins—there is a bit more to it. We must be ready for such a great gift, and so to gain a plenary indulgence one must, along with the act attached to the indulgence, fulfill three conditions: sacramental Confession (within twenty days), Holy Communion (on the day of the act, if possible), and prayer for the pope's intentions (an Our Father and Hail Mary or other prayers). One sacramental Confession suffices for several plenary indulgences, but each plenary indulgence requires its own Communion and prayer for the Holy Father's intentions.

There is a final requirement in the gaining of a plenary indulgence, and that is a detachment from all sin, even venial sin. This means that you wish not to sin and you will to prefer God to everything else. This does not mean that you feel a complete aversion to all sin. The important point here is that you have a detachment in your will. Since the will is invisible and rather difficult to see, a handy way of detaching from all sin—or making a worthy attempt—is to say the Act of Contrition with special attention when you get to the words, "I detest all my sins because of Thy just punishments, *but most of all because they offend Thee, my God, who art all good and deserving of all my love.*"

These are the conditions, but what about the acts to which a plenary indulgence is attached? There is a little book called *New Regulations on Indulgences,* and a slightly larger book called *The Handbook of Indulgences: Norms and Grants* (which

contains *Indulgentiarum Doctrina* as well). Both books spell
out carefully what the acts are that the Church proposes for
gaining indulgences, both plenary and partial.

Many plenary indulgences are assigned to a particular day of
the year—for instance, the plenary indulgence attached to visiting a cemetery and praying for the dead, which can be gained
each day from November 1 through November 8. There are
many such opportunities to gain plenary indulgences on specific
days, and the two books just mentioned give all the particulars.

Of special interest, though, are the four plenary indulgences that can be gained every day of the year (though only
one per day). When the usual conditions are met, a daily
plenary indulgence may be obtained by (1) recitation of the
Rosary in a church or family, religious community, or pious
association; (2) making the fourteen Stations of the Cross in
a church; (3) adoration of the Blessed Sacrament for a half
hour; and (4) reading Sacred Scripture for a half hour.

And what about that strange proviso I mentioned earlier
regarding the day of death? For as long as I've known about
it, this has struck me as the most maternal of Holy Mother
Church's indulgences to us. I quote from *The Handbook of
Indulgences: Norms and Grants* (no. 28 of the Grants):

> Priests who minister the sacraments to the Christian faithful
> who are in a life-and-death situation should not neglect to
> impart to them the apostolic blessing, with its attached indul-
> gence. But if a priest cannot be present, Holy Mother Church
> lovingly grants such persons who are rightly disposed a plenary
> indulgence to be obtained in articulo mortis, at the approach
> of death, provided they regularly prayed in some way during
> their lifetime. The use of a crucifix or a cross is recommended
> in obtaining this plenary indulgence. In such a situation the
> three usual conditions required in order to gain a plenary
> indulgence [Confession, Communion, and prayer for the Holy

Father's intentions] are substituted for by the condition "provided they regularly prayed in some way." The Christian faithful can obtain the plenary indulgence mentioned here as death approaches even if they had already obtained another plenary indulgence that same day.

The mercy of God is beyond our imagining, but through divine revelation and the ministry of the Church, He tries to give us a good picture of it! And now you know what every Catholic should know about indulgences and Christ's maternal love for your dear soul.

The last thing you need to know is that there is no need to fear God—He loves you and made you for eternal happiness with Him in heaven. And when you get there? Then you finally will know absolutely everything a Catholic should know. As St. Augustine promises, "How great, how lovely, how certain is the knowledge of all things there, with no error and no trouble, where the wisdom of God shall be imbibed at its very source with no difficulty and utmost happiness!"[9]

---

9   Jill Haak Adels, *The Wisdom of the Saints* (New York: Oxford University Press, 1989), 201.

Chapter 21

A Treasury of Catholic
Prayers and Lists

Build yourself a cell in your heart and retire there to pray.

—St. Catherine of Siena

Morning Offering

Dear Jesus, through the Immaculate Heart of Mary, I offer Thee my every thought, work, action, joy, and suffering of this day, in union with the Holy Sacrifice of the Mass throughout the world. I desire to gain every merit and indulgence I can and offer them, together with myself, to Mary Immaculate, that she may apply them to the interests of Thy most Sacred Heart.

Our Father

Our Father, who art in heaven, hallowed be Thy name.
Thy kingdom come, Thy will be done on earth as it is in
    heaven.
Give us this day our daily bread and forgive us our trespasses,
as we forgive those who trespass against us.
And lead us not into temptation, but deliver us from evil.
    Amen.

Hail Mary

Hail Mary, full of grace, the Lord is with thee.
Blessed art thou amongst women and blessed is the fruit of
    thy womb, Jesus.
Holy Mary, Mother of God,
pray for us sinners, now, and at the hour of our death. Amen.

Glory Be (Doxology)

Glory be to the Father, and to the Son, and to the Holy Spirit.
As it was in the beginning, is now, and ever shall be, world
    without end. Amen.

Act of Contrition

O my God, I am heartily sorry for having offended Thee, and
I detest all my sins because of Thy just punishments, but most
of all because they offend Thee, my God, who art all good and
deserving of all my love. I firmly resolve, with the help of Thy
grace, to confess my sins, to do penance, and to amend my
life. Amen.

Apostles' Creed

I believe in God, the Father almighty, Creator of heaven and
    earth.
And in Jesus Christ, His only Son, our Lord,
who was conceived by the Holy Spirit,
born of the Virgin Mary,
suffered under Pontius Pilate,
was crucified, died, and was buried.
He descended into hell;
the third day He rose again from the dead;
He ascended into heaven,
and is seated at the right hand of God,

the Father almighty;
from there shall come to judge the living and the dead.
I believe in the Holy Spirit,
the holy catholic Church,
the communion of saints,
the forgiveness of sins,
the resurrection of the body
and life everlasting. Amen.

Nicene Creed

I believe in one God, the Father almighty,
maker of heaven and earth, of all things visible and invisible.
I believe in one Lord Jesus Christ,
the Only Begotten Son of God, born of the Father before all
   ages.
God from God, Light from Light,
true God from true God,
begotten, not made, consubstantial with the Father;
through Him all things were made.
For us men and for our salvation He came down from heaven,
and by the Holy Spirit was incarnate of the Virgin Mary,
and became man.
For our sake He was crucified under Pontius Pilate,
He suffered death and was buried,
and rose again on the third day
in accordance with the Scriptures.
He ascended into heaven and is seated at the right hand of
   the Father.
He will come again in glory to judge the living and the dead
and His kingdom will have no end.
I believe in the Holy Spirit, the Lord, the giver of life,
who proceeds from the Father and the Son,
who with the Father and the Son is adored and glorified,
who has spoken through the prophets.

I believe in one, holy, catholic and apostolic Church.
I confess one Baptism for the forgiveness of sins
and I look forward to the resurrection of the dead
and the life of the world to come. Amen.

Holy Spirit Prayer (*Veni Sancte Spiritus*)

Come, Holy Spirit, fill the hearts of Thy faithful and enkindle
    in them the fire of Thy love.
Send forth Thy Spirit and they shall be created,
and Thou shalt renew the face of the earth.
Let us pray.
O God, who didst instruct the hearts of the faithful by the
    light of the Holy Spirit,
grant us in that same Spirit to be truly wise, and ever to rejoice
    in His consolation.
Through Christ, our Lord. Amen.

Memorare

Remember, O most gracious Virgin Mary,
that never was it known that anyone who fled to thy protection,
implored thy help, or sought thy intercession was left unaided.
Inspired by this confidence, O Virgin of Virgins, my Mother,
to thee do I come, to thee do I call.
O Mother of the Word Incarnate,
despise not my petitions, but in thy mercy hear and answer
    me. Amen.

Guardian Angel Prayer

Angel of God, my guardian dear,
to whom God's love commits me here,
ever this day, be at my side,
to light, to guard, to rule and guide.

St. Michael Prayer

St. Michael the Archangel,
defend us in battle.
Be our protection against the wickedness and snares of the
    devil.
May God rebuke him, we humbly pray;
and do thou, O Prince of the Heavenly Host,
by the power of God,
cast into hell Satan and all the evil spirits
who prowl about the world seeking the ruin of souls. Amen.

Prayer to St. Raphael

O Raphael, lead us toward those we are waiting for, those
who are waiting for us: Raphael, Angel of happy meeting, lead
us by the hand toward those we are looking for. May all our
movements be guided by your Light and transfigured with
your joy.

Angel, guide of Tobias, lay the request we now address to
you at the feet of Him on whose unveiled Face you are privi-
leged to gaze. Lonely and tired, crushed by the separations and
sorrows of life, we feel the need of calling you and of pleading
for the protection of your wings, so that we may not be as
strangers in the province of joy, all ignorant of the concerns
of our country. Remember the weak, you who are strong, you
whose home lies beyond the region of thunder, in a land that
is always peaceful, always serene and bright with the resplendent glory of God. Amen.

Hail Holy Queen (*Salve Regina*)

Hail holy Queen, Mother of mercy, our life, our sweetness,
and our hope. To thee do we cry, poor banished children of
Eve. To thee do we send up our sighs, mourning and weeping

in this valley of tears. Turn then, most gracious Advocate, thine eyes of mercy toward us. And after this our exile show unto us the blessed fruit of thy womb, Jesus. O clement, O loving, O sweet Virgin Mary.

Pray for us, O holy Mother of God,

That we may be made worthy of the promises of Christ.

Fatima Prayer (after each decade of the Rosary)

O my Jesus, forgive us our sins, save us from the fires of hell, and lead all souls to heaven, especially those in most need of Thy mercy.

Prayer of St. Thomas Aquinas before Communion

Almighty, everlasting God, look down in mercy upon me, Thy servant, who now again draw near to the most Holy Sacrament of Thine only begotten Son, Our Lord Jesus Christ. I approach as one who is sick, to the physician of life; as one unclean, to the fountain of mercy; as one blind, to the light of eternal brightness; as one poor and needy, to the Lord of heaven and earth. I implore Thee, therefore, out of the abundance of Thy boundless mercy, that Thou wouldst vouchsafe to heal my sickness, to wash away my defilement, to give sight to my eyes, to enrich my poverty, and to clothe my nakedness, that I may receive the bread of angels, the King of kings, the Lord of lords, with such reverence and humility, such contrition and devotion, such purity and faith, such purpose and intention, as may tend to the salvation of my soul.

Grant to me, I beseech Thee, not only to receive the sacrament of the Body and Blood of the Lord, but to profit by its substance and virtue. O God most merciful, grant me the grace to receive the Body of Thine only-begotten Son, Jesus Christ, Our Lord, which He took of the Virgin Mary, in such wise, that I may be found worthy to be incorporated into His mystical body, and forevermore to be numbered among His members.

O Father most loving, I am about to welcome into my heart Thine own beloved Son, hidden under His sacramental veil: may it, in Thy great goodness, be mine, in the end, for all eternity face-to-face to gaze upon Him: Who with Thee liveth and reigneth, in the unity of the Holy Spirit, God, world without end. Amen.

Litany of Loreto (Litany of Our Lady)

V. Lord, have mercy.
R. *Christ have mercy.*
V. Lord have mercy. Christ hear us.
R. *Christ graciously hear us.*

God the Father of heaven, *have mercy on us.*
God the Son, Redeemer of the world, *have mercy on us.*
God the Holy Spirit, *have mercy on us.*
Holy Trinity, one God, *have mercy on us.*

Holy Mary, *pray for us.*
Holy Mother of God, *pray for us.*
Holy Virgin of Virgins, *[etc.]*
Mother of Christ,
Mother of divine grace,
Mother most pure,
Mother most chaste,
Mother inviolate,
Mother undefiled,
Mother most amiable,
Mother most admirable,
Mother of good Counsel,
Mother of our Creator,
Mother of our Savior,
Virgin most prudent,

Virgin most venerable,
Virgin most renowned,
Virgin most powerful,
Virgin most merciful,
Virgin most faithful,
Mirror of justice,
Seat of wisdom,
Cause of our joy,
Spiritual vessel,
Vessel of honor,
Singular vessel of devotion,
Mystical rose,
Tower of David,
Tower of ivory,
House of gold,
Ark of the covenant,
Gate of heaven,
Morning star,
Health of the sick,
Refuge of sinners,
Comforter of the afflicted,
Help of Christians,
Queen of Angels,
Queen of Patriarchs,
Queen of Prophets,
Queen of Apostles,
Queen of Martyrs,
Queen of Confessors,
Queen of Virgins,
Queen of all Saints,
Queen conceived without Original Sin,
Queen assumed into heaven,
Queen of the most holy Rosary,
Queen of peace,

V. Lamb of God, who takest away the sins of the world,
R. *Spare us, O Lord.*
V. Lamb of God, who takest away the sins of the world,
R. *Graciously hear us, O Lord.*
V. Lamb of God, who takest away the sins of the world,
R. *Have mercy on us.*

V. Pray for us, O holy Mother of God,
R. *That we may be made worthy of the promises of Christ.*

V. Let us pray. Grant, we beseech Thee, O Lord God, that we Thy servants may enjoy perpetual health of mind and body, and by the glorious intercession of blessed Mary, ever Virgin, may we be freed from present sorrow, and rejoice in eternal happiness. Through Christ our Lord.
R. *Amen.*

How to Say the Rosary

Make the Sign of the Cross.

Opening Prayers

Begin with the Apostles' Creed on the crucifix.
On the first bead after the crucifix, say the Our Father.
On each of the next three beads, say a Hail Mary.
On the fifth bead, say the Glory Be and then the Fatima Prayer
    (O my Jesus, etc.)

Main Body of the Rosary

On the large beads before each group of ten beads, say an Our Father.
On each of the ten beads (a decade), say a Hail Mary.
After each decade (ten beads), say the Glory Be and the Fatima Prayer.

Closing Prayers

After you have said five decades and are back at the beginning, say the Hail Holy Queen. Other prayers commonly said after the Rosary are the St. Michael Prayer, and an Our Father, Hail Mary, and Glory Be for the Holy Father's intentions, to gain an indulgence. Also an Act of Contrition may be said to intend detachment from all sin.

The Joyful Mysteries (suggested for Monday and Saturday)

The Annunciation by the Archangel Gabriel to Mary, who is chosen to be the Mother of God

The Visitation of Our Lady, to her cousin St. Elizabeth

The Nativity, or Birth of Our Lord, in Bethlehem

The Presentation of Our Lord in the Temple

The Finding in the Temple of the Boy Jesus, teaching the doctors of the Jewish law

The Luminous Mysteries or Mysteries of Light (suggested for Thursday)

The Baptism of the Lord by St. John the Baptist

The Wedding Feast at Cana

The Preaching of the Coming of the Kingdom of God

The Transfiguration of Our Lord

The Institution of the Eucharist at the Last Supper

The Sorrowful Mysteries (suggested for Tuesday and Friday)

The Agony in the Garden

The Scourging at the Pillar

The Crowning with Thorns

The Carrying of the Cross
The Crucifixion and Death of Our Lord

The Glorious Mysteries (suggested for Wednesday and Sunday)

The Resurrection of Jesus from the dead on Easter
The Ascension of Our Lord, forty days after His Resurrection
The Descent of the Holy Spirit on Our Lady and the Apostles
    on Pentecost
The Assumption of Our Lady, body and soul, into heaven
The Coronation of Mary, as Queen of Heaven and Earth

The Divine Mercy Chaplet

The Chaplet of Mercy is recited using ordinary rosary beads
of five decades.

Opening Prayers

Make the Sign of the Cross: In the name of the Father, and of
    the Son, and of the Holy Spirit. Amen.
Say the Our Father.
Say the Hail Mary.
Say the Apostles' Creed.

Main Body of the Rosary

On the large beads (leading into each decade of ten beads)
say: Eternal Father, I offer you the Body and Blood, Soul and
Divinity, of Your Dearly Beloved Son, Our Lord, Jesus Christ,
in atonement for our sins and those of the whole world.

On the ten small beads of each decade say: For the sake of
His sorrowful passion, have mercy on us and on the whole
world.

Closing Prayers

Conclude with the Trisagion, repeating it three times: Holy
God, Holy Mighty One, Holy Immortal One, have mercy on
us and on the whole world.

The Ten Commandments

1. I am the LORD your God: you shall not have strange gods
   before me.
2. You shall not take the name of the LORD your God in
   vain.
3. Remember to keep holy the LORD's Day.
4. Honor your father and your mother.
5. You shall not kill.
6. You shall not commit adultery.
7. You shall not steal.
8. You shall not bear false witness against your neighbor.
9. You shall not covet your neighbor's wife.
10. You shall not covet your neighbor's goods.

The Five Precepts of the Church

1. Attend Mass on Sundays and on holy days of obligation,
   and rest from servile labor.
2. Confess your sins at least once a year.
3. Receive the Sacrament of the Eucharist at least during the
   Easter season.
4. Observe the days of fasting and abstinence established by
   the Church.
5. Help provide for the needs of the Church.

The Twenty-One Ecumenical Councils

1. First Council of Nicaea (325)
2. First Council of Constantinople (381)

3. Council of Ephesus (431)
4. Council of Chalcedon (451)
5. Second Council of Constantinople (553)
6. Third Council of Constantinople (680–681)
7. Second Council of Nicaea (787)
8. Fourth Council of Constantinople (869)
9. First Lateran Council (1123)
10. Second Lateran Council (1139)
11. Third Lateran Council (1179)
12. Fourth Lateran Council (1215)
13. First Council of Lyons (1245)
14. Second Council of Lyons (1274)
15. Council of Vienne (1311–1313)
16. Council of Constance (1414–1418)
17. Council of Basle/Ferrara/Florence (1431–1439)
18. Fifth Lateran Council (1512–1517)
19. Council of Trent (1545–1563)
20. First Vatican Council (1869–1870)
21. Second Vatican Council (1962–1965)

The Doctors of the Church

St. Athanasius (ca. 297–373), Father of Orthodoxy

St. Ephrem the Syrian (ca. 306–373), Father of Hymnody

St. Cyril of Jerusalem (ca. 315–386), Doctor of Catechesis

St. Hilary of Poitiers (ca. 315–368), The Athanasius of the West

St. Basil the Great (ca. 329–379), Father of Eastern Monasticism

St. Gregory Nanzianzen (ca. 330–390), The Theologian, The Christian Demosthenes

St. Ambrose (ca. 340–397), Patron of the Veneration of Mary

St. Jerome (ca. 343–420), Father of Biblical Science

St. John Chrysostom (ca. 347–407), Golden-Mouthed, Doctor of the Eucharist

St. Augustine (ca. 354–430) Doctor of Grace, Doctor of Doctors

St. Cyril of Alexandria (ca. 376–444), Doctor of the Incarnation, Seal of the Fathers

Pope St. Leo the Great (ca. 400–461), Doctor of the Unity of the Church

St. Peter Chrysologus (ca. 400–450), Golden-Worded

Pope St. Gregory the Great (ca. 540–604)

St. Isidore of Seville (ca. 560–636)

St. Bede the Venerable (ca. 673–735), Father of English History

St. John Damascene (ca. 675–749), Doctor of the Assumption

St. Gregory Narek (951–1003)

St. Peter Damian (1007–1072)

St. Anselm of Canterbury (1033–1109), Father of Scholasticism

St. Bernard of Clairvaux (ca. 1090–1153), Mellifluous Doctor

St. Hildegard of Bingen (1098–1179)

St. Anthony of Padua (1195–1231), Evangelical Doctor

St. Albert the Great (ca. 1200–1280), Universal Doctor

St. Bonaventure (ca. 1217–1274), Seraphic Doctor

St. Thomas Aquinas (1225–1274), Angelic Doctor, Common Doctor

St. Catherine of Siena (c. 1347–1380), Seraphic Virgin

St. John of Avila (1500–1569)

St. Teresa of Avila (1515–1582), Doctor of Prayer

St. Peter Canisius (1521–1597), Doctor of the Catechism

St. Robert Bellarmine (1542–1621), Prince of Apologists

St. John of the Cross (1542–1591), Doctor of Mystical Theology

St. Lawrence of Brindisi (1559–1619), Apostolic Doctor

St. Francis de Sales (1567–1622), Patron of Catholic Writers

St. Alphonsus Liguori (1696–1787), Prince of Moralists

St. Thérèse of Lisieux (1873–1897), Doctor of the Little Way